D1569850

Austrian Economics: An Anthology

Compiled and edited by
Bettina Bien Greaves

Foundation for Economic Education
Irvington-on-Hudson, NY 10533

Austrian Economics: An Anthology

Copyright © 1996 by the Foundation for Economic Education

The Foundation for Economic Education, Inc.
30 South Broadway
Irvington-on-Hudson, NY 10533
(914) 591-7230

Publisher's Cataloging in Publication
(Prepared by Quality Books, Inc.)

Austrian economics: an anthology / compiled and edited by Bettina
    Bien Greaves.
    p. cm.
    Includes bibliographical references and index.
    ISBN: 1-57246-056-3

    1. Austrian school of economists. 2. Economics—History.
I. Greaves, Bettina Bien.

HB98.A98   1996   330.15'7
                                    QBI96-40330

Library of Congress Catalog Card Number: 96-078763

Cover design by Beth R. Bowlby
Manufactured in the United States of America

The body of economic knowledge is an essential element in the structure of human civilization; it is the foundation upon which modern industrialism and all moral, intellectual, technological, and therapeutical achievements of the last centuries have been built. It rests with men whether they will make the proper use of the rich treasure with which this knowledge provides them or whether they will leave it unused. But if they fail to take the best advantage of it and disregard its teachings and warnings, they will not annul economics; they will stamp out society and the human race.

LUDWIG VON MISES, Human Action (1949)

Table of Contents

Acknowledgments   vii

Introduction by Bettina Bien Greaves   1

HISTORY

1. The Austrian Economists and Their View of Value
   by James Bonar (1888)   11

2. Economics at Berlin and Vienna
   by H. R. Seager (1893)   33

3. Carl Menger and the Austrian School of Economics
   by Ludwig von Mises (*Neue Freie Presse*, 1929)   47

4. The Historical Setting of the Austrian School
   of Economics
   by Ludwig von Mises (1969)   53

5. Austrian School of Economics
   by Ludwig von Mises (1962)   77

EPISTEMOLOGY

6. The Austrian Economists
   by Eugen von Böhm-Bawerk (1891)   85

7. Remarks on the Fundamental Problem of the
   Subjective Theory of Value
   by Ludwig von Mises (1928)   105

8. On the Development of the Subjective Theory of Value
   by Ludwig von Mises (1933)   119

9. The Epistemological Problems
   by Ludwig von Mises (excerpts from
   Human Action, 1949)   137

References for Further Study   159

Index   163

Acknowledgments

This book would not be complete without acknowledging the support of Dr. Hans F. Sennholz, President of the Foundation for Economic Education. Also the help of Miss Janette Brown for entering all these articles into the computer, as well as Mrs. Beth Hoffman for exceptional editorial assistance.

I should also like to give credit to Professor Richard Ebeling of Hillsdale College (Hillsdale, Michigan) for locating, in the course of his research in Vienna into the history of the Austrian School of Economics, the early articles by James Bonar (1888) and H. R. Seager (1893), and for sending me copies.

—BBG

Introduction

As a participant for many years in Ludwig von Mises' New York University graduate seminar in economic theory, I was distressed by the neglect of the "Austrian School of Economics" among college and university professors and in textbooks on the history of economic thought. This book attempts to fill that gap to some extent. It tells something of the step-by-step development of the Austrian school, its theories and their gradual dissemination. In recent years, the influence of the Austrian school has been increasing and its explanations of economic matters are being more seriously treated in colleges and universities. Thus the ideas of the Austrian school are beginning to have some impact on economic thinking and even on government policy in some countries.

* * * * * * * * * *

By the end of the 18th century, economics was recognized as a special discipline for study, apart from the natural sciences and moral philosophy. The economists of that period, later known as Classical economists, recognized a regularity in interpersonal relationships. Like scientists throughout the ages who sought the truth in their respective fields, those early economists tried to understand and explain the regularity they noted in the actions of men in relation to other men and to the world around them. They considered their special field of study to be that of production, trade, commerce, and business. In the attempt to explain as much as they could about these phenomena, they analyzed the forces which they saw as responsible for production and trade—land, labor, and capital. Among other things, they concluded that market prices arose out of the interplay of supply and demand on the market. But their explanation, depending as it did on holistic concepts, fell short of explaining specific prices. For instance, they couldn't understand why something useful like a loaf of bread or a hod of coal cost much less on the market than an ounce of gold or a piece of jewelry that filled no urgent human need. Moreover, they left out of account immaterial or "uneconomic" items and the "unproductive" services of lawyers, doctors, opera singers, musicians, etc. Thus the analyses of the Classicals failed to offer a complete explanation of all interpersonal

1

relationships; they could not explain satisfactorily the formation of specific prices.

It was not until a century or so later that a new generation of economists pinpointed the error in the reasoning of the Classical economists. The breakthrough came when Carl Menger (1840–1921), born within the boundary of what was then the huge conglomerate of the Austro-Hungarian Empire, clearly explained the theory of subjective value and marginal utility. In doing this, Menger rejected the holism of the Classicals. He dismissed land, labor, capital, supply, and demand as holistic concepts and traced market prices to the actions of individuals. Value theory, as expounded by Menger and further elaborated by two of his Austrian-born successors, Eugen von Böhm-Bawerk (1851–1914) and Friedrich von Wieser (1851–1926), proved the "Open sesame!" to understanding all economic problems. Carl Menger's *Principles of Economics* (1871; first English translation, 1950) and Eugen Böhm-Bawerk's chapters on "Value and Price" in his major work, *Capital and Interest* (3rd edition, 1914; English translation, 1959), have become classics. It was because of the contributions of these Austrian-born economists that the subjective, marginal utility, value theory was later labeled "Austrian."

The new Austrian methodology, which traced market prices to the actions of individuals was known as methodological individualism. It pointed out that market prices, as well as of all other economic phenomena, rested unequivocally on the decisions, preferences, and subjective values of individuals. Thus the market price of a particular item (a loaf of bread) depends, not on the usefulness of the category of goods of which it is one specimen (food), nor on the value of a collection of such specimens (the baker's stock of bread), but rather on the satisfaction the specific individual involved hopes to derive from that particular quantity of the good (one loaf of bread) or service (relief of hunger) at a particular time and place. That is, the market price of a particular item depends on the expected "marginal utility" of the unit concerned to a specific individual. Menger expressed it very simply: "[T]he value of each quantity of goods is equal to the importance of the satisfactions that depend on it." (*Principles,* p. 135) In this way, by tracing market prices back to the subjective values of individuals, to their ideas, decisions, preferences, and actions, the Austrians resolved the Classicals' "paradox of value."

The new methodology adopted by these early Austrian economists, as well as by later "Austrian" economists—all around the world, irrespective of national origin—rejected not only the holistic methodology of their Classical predecessors, but also the historical method of the

German Historical school, the dominant economic school of their day. A heated methodological controversy developed in the 1890s, a debate which gained notoriety as the *Methodenstreit*. The Austrians pointed to the sharp distinction between (1) economic history, the data and statistics describing past events which their German contemporaries—historicists, positivists, empiricists, institutionalists, collectivists—presented as economics, and (2) the logical science of economics. Economic history, economic statistics, the Austrians argued, was the study of what men had done at certain times and places in the past. The science of economics was a universal science which used reason, logic, methodological individualism, to analyze and understand the actions of men, all men, at any time, everywhere.

Ludwig von Mises (1881–1973), who became the leading spokesman of the next generation of Austrian economists, had known Menger and studied with Böhm-Bawerk. Mises carried economic reason and logic a step farther; he broadened the field of study by incorporating economics into the more general science of praxeology, the science of all human action. Economics in the narrower sense, the study of the actions of men on the market (catallactics), is a subsidiary of praxeology. Praxeological theories are developed by reasoning logically from fundamental a priori categories. Thus economics, like praxeology, is a logical science and its methodological individualism derives logically from the a priori of action.

This book brings the development of Austrian economics down through Mises. He left Austria for Switzerland in 1934 and in 1940 fled war-torn Europe and came to the United States. He brought with him to this country his indomitable spirit, courage, and determination to continue his studies and his teaching. His books and lectures became his platform.

The decades after World War II constituted the nadir of Austrian economics in this country and throughout the world. Academia was dominated by Keynesianism, historicism, positivism, and collectivism and was not particularly hospitable to Austrian ideas, or to Mises. However, some of his friends subsidized his appointment as Visiting Professor at New York University Graduate School of Business Administration and he taught there from 1945 to 1969. The university let Mises teach, but otherwise they pretty much ignored him. One student reported that NYU administration officials actively tried to discourage him from taking Mises' course; it was not economics, they said; it was a "religion." Nevertheless, Austrian methodological individualism was kept alive during these decades primarily through Mises—his NYU seminar, the Foundation for Economic Education for which he became economic adviser, his teachings, and his books. The Mont Pèlerin Society, composed of free market minded academicians and businessmen, which had been founded in 1947 by Mises and his fellow Austrian, Professor F. A. Hayek, helped to some extent internationally.

Most of the participants in Mises' NYU graduate seminar were not academicians. However, many of the regulars became serious students of Austrian economics and went on to contribute something, each in his or her own way, to Austrian economics. Some became college professors. Some worked for free-market think tanks. Some were journalists. Some taught. Many of them followed Mises' recommendation and wrote books. Among the regular NYU seminar participants in alphabetical order, were Bettina (Bien) Greaves, Percy L. Greaves, Jr., Henry Hazlitt, Joseph Keckeissen, Israel M. Kirzner, George Koether, Toshio Murata of Japan, William H. Peterson, George Reisman, Murray N. Rothbard, Hans F. Sennholz, Mary (Homan) Sennholz, and Louis M. Spadaro.* Two other "Austrians" should be mentioned—Britisher W. H. Hutt and German-born Ludwig M. Lachmann—both of whom arrived in this country from South Africa.

During the post-World War II decades, Austrian economics was practically an underground movement, but it is gradually gaining some recognition. Mises died in 1973. In 1974, F. A. Hayek, Mises' close friend and associate from Vienna, was awarded the Nobel prize in economics. Also in 1974, an Institute for Humane Studies conference at South Royalton, Vermont, featuring lectures by Kirzner, Rothbard, and Lachmann, renewed interest in Austrian economics. Since then many young people have been introduced to the subject, countless discussions and debates have been held and many "Austrian" books and articles have been published. Many of this new generation of "Austrians" began studying economics as students of Mises' NYU seminar participants.

---

*Over the years quite a few other persons attended Mises' NYU Seminar as visitors or for one or two semesters. Many who went on to help keep Austrian ideas alive through their various activities and contacts should be mentioned: Beverly (Kline) Anderson, Robert G. Anderson, Manuel Ayau of Guatemala, Alberto Benegas Lynch, Sr. and Jr., both of Argentina, George W. Bishop, Walter Block, Henry M. Boettinger, Herbert Bracey, William Burkett, Roy Childs, J. Vincent Cordero, Richard Cornuelle, Mallory Cross, Rev. John F. Davis, Frank T. Dierson, Robert J. Dobson, Richard L. Fruin, Robert Guanieri, Ronald S. Hertz, Robert Hessen, Isidor Hodes, Wayne J. Holman, Hiram J. Honea, Hugh King, David L. Jarrett, J. Ranney Johnson, Leonard Liggio, Father M. Mansfield, Edwin McDowell, Father McInnis, Luis Montes de Oca of Mexico, Laurence S. Moss, Agustin Navarro of Mexico, Vincent A. Novo, Frederick C. Nymeyer, Ralph Raico, John R. Rohrs, Robert J. Smith, Allan J. Trumbull, John van Eck, Gustavo Velasco of Mexico, and Fuchow Wang of Formosa.

* * * * * * * * * *

The early Austrian economists and their successors, under the guidance of Mises, recognized a sharp distinction between the methodology of history, the methodology of the physical sciences, and the methodology of economics. The great contribution of the Austrians is their methodology; they use logic to develop methodological individualism. They view man as a thinking, acting person, a person with a mind, subjective values, and many wants, who is always striving to improve his or her situation. "Austrians" place *individuals* at the center of the economic system. They realize that it is only by studying the conscious, purposive actions of individuals, which reveal their decisions, choices, preferences, and values, that one may understand the relationship of acting men to the physical world and to other men. And it is only by studying the actions of acting men that one can understand and explain such economic phenomena as prices, wages, costs, production, profits, losses, money, banking, economic calculation, economic booms and busts, and so on ad infinitum, as well as the immaterial services and other values which Classical economists dismissed as "uneconomic."

Advocates of applying an empirical or statistical methodology to economics are not theoreticians; therefore, they are not economists in the Austrian sense; they are economic historians. They observe and describe economic phenomena of the past but do not *explain* them. They deal with economic averages and aggregates and, in the process, they ignore the most significant factor, that an average or aggregate is the composite outcome of the conscious, purposive acts of many individuals. They talk about "forests" and forget the "trees." Their methodology is historical, not logical.

* * * * * * * * * *

Many advocates of empiricism, historicism, or positivism maintain that the test of a scientific truth is whether or not it may be used as the basis for prediction. They compile massive data on recent economic phenomena in the hope that in time they will have enough statistics to enable them to discover an economic law or theory. They look for fixed and meaningful mathematical correlations among various aggregates. They consider some statistical aggregates to be "indicators," because they are supposed to give some "indication" as to future developments. However, no economic statistic nor any accumulation of many economic statistics can ever yield an economic theory or law. To be sure, statistical extrapolations may be made, and such extrapolations are sometimes called "predictions." But any such extrapolation is not based on statistics alone; rather it is based on a theory, and a rather unreliable theory at that, the theory that current trends will continue. No extrapolation can say anything about how long any particular current trend will continue, nor if, as, or when it will change. But one thing is certain: present trends *will* change. History is always change. No one can learn the future from the past.

Predictions *are* possible, however, *in the field of logical economics,* although not on the basis of history. Predictions are possible on the basis of "Austrian" theory and an understanding of the universal and eternal principles of human action. But such predictions can only be qualitative, not quantitative. For instance, we can predict that, given human nature and the world of limited resources, time, and energy in which we live, goods and services in great demand will be relatively more valuable on the market than those not so urgently demanded, although we cannot say how much more valuable. By that same token, we can predict that in a society which protects private property and allows potential producers freedom to experiment, some entrepreneurs will try to expand production of the desired goods and services. And we can predict that, other things being equal, if demand for these items falls, so will their market value, and thus also the incentive of would-be entrepreneurs to expand their production.

Another prediction we can make is that, if the quantity of money is increased while the demand for it remains the same or falls, prices generally will tend to rise, although not all prices will rise at the same time or to the same extent. The prices of some goods or services may even fall if buyers refuse to buy them.

* * * * * * * * * *

The methodological individualism of the Austrians has proven extremely fruitful in helping to develop and explain economic phenomena. By reasoning logically, step-by-step, on the basis of the fundamental a priori, action axiom, the "Austrians" have developed the logical science of economics. They have explained how the different values held by different individuals lead to specialization, interpersonal cooperation, and trade. They have explained the role of private property and the importance of time. They have explained money and how it originates as the most marketable commodity in a community. They have explained money's impact on prices, trade, exchange rates, as well as on patterns of production. They have explained interest rates, inflation, banking, credit expansion, even "stagflation" and economic booms and busts. They have shown how the hope of profit and the fear of loss guide individuals and inspire entrepreneurs to serve consumers, reduce waste, and channel resources into their most urgent uses.

Economic methodology may appear just what one might expect of the "dismal science" of economics, dull, uninteresting, and unrelated to everyday life. Yet it is extremely relevant today, especially to government policy. It was the teachings of the German historicists that led the German people to believe that government had the power to control and regulate the economy, thus paving the way for Hitler, Nazism, omnipotent government, and war. On the other hand, the teachings of Austrian economics show the way to peace and prosperity.

Austrian economics explains that there are economic laws which no government can ignore, set aside, or nullify. With its understanding of methodological individualism, it demonstrates that government must acknowledge these economic laws and try not to violate them if its people are to live in peace. Austrian insight explains how government controls and regulations hamper their efforts. If individuals are to produce efficiently and effectively, they must be free and independent to pursue their own personal values and peaceful goals.

In his magnum opus, *Human Action*, Mises developed economic theory logically and scientifically. He set forth with extreme care and rigid logic the epistemology, the methodology, of Austrian economics. Yet he could not completely conceal his emotions. In the very last sentence of his book, he revealed the depth of his conviction that the recognition of Austrian methodology was essential for civilization's survival. If men fail to take advantage of the economic knowledge developed by the praxeological law of human action, he wrote, if they "disregard its teachings and warnings, they will not annul economics; they will stamp out society and the human race." (*Human Action*, p. 885)

Granted men have limited knowledge; they are not infallible or omniscient; they cannot know the future. Still we can predict with certainty that if men are free to pursue their various ends in peace, cooperate with others as they think best, so long as they do not use force or fraud to interfere with the equal rights of others, there will be a tendency for everyone to be better off. On the other hand, coercive government intervention disrupts peaceful economic development and may lead to interpersonal and/or international strife. This insight, derived from an understanding of Austrian theory, logic, and methodological individualism, distinguishes Austrian economics from other schools of economic thought.

* * * * * * * * * *

The laws and principles of the physical sciences are universal, eternal, and remain the same throughout the ages. The physical sciences of astronomy, biology, chemistry, physics, physiology, geology, mathematics, etc., have not changed since the days of the Egyptian pharaohs. Moreover, they are true everywhere throughout the world. Of course, our mastery of these sciences has increased with study, exploration, and improved technology, thus expanding dramatically our knowledge of the physical world, the human body, the universe, the stars, and the planets.

The situation is the same with respect to the science of economics. The laws of human action are not limited to any particular time or to any particular place any more than are the laws of the physical sciences. They are the same in Austria as in Nigeria, Singapore, and the United States. They are the same for the rich and the poor, the Nazis, Communists, liberals or libertarians, and the Marxian proletarians as well as for members of the bourgeois "class." The laws and principles of human action apply always and everywhere, given the same conditions, wherever there are living, acting human beings.

If the laws of human action are universal and eternal, why then do we speak of Austrian economics? Out of respect for the Austrian "founding fathers" who developed the subjective, marginal utility, theory of value, basis of the logical science of economics. And also to distinguish our science from historical and statistical economic doctrines such as positivism and institutionalism.

* * * * * * * * * *

A number of chapters in this anthology describe the early development of Austrian economics and the 19th-century methodological struggle, the *Methodenstreit*. Others explain Austrian value theory and methodological individualism, demonstrating how all economic phenomena derive from the actions of individuals. Individuals may act alone, of course, and/or in cooperation or competition with others. The economic transactions that result may be simple or complex, time-consuming, technologically complicated, coordinated, interrelated, and/or integrated with one another. However, in the last analysis, they can always be traced back to the ideas, preferences, choices, actions, and mistakes of the various individuals participating. This is the Austrian contribution to the universal and eternal science of economics.

—BETTINA BIEN GREAVES

HISTORY

The Austrian Economists and Their View of Value[1]

by James Bonar

The Ricardian doctrine of value has had its share of the general sifting of cardinal principles which has been at work in England and abroad for the last two generations. No one would now agree with Mill that there is nothing in the laws of value which remains for any future writer to clear up.[2] In England, the criticisms of Jevons and others have made a deep impression. The positive doctrines of Jevons have not had an equal success, but they have fared somewhat better on the Continent. And, in Austria, a body of doctrines substantially identical with those of Jevons have become the tenets of a strong school, which has made Austria more prominent in economical discussion than she has been for at least a century. There seems to be something of the same intellectual rivalry between Austria and her German neighbors as between America and England.

Carl Menger,[3] Friedrich von Wieser[4] and Eugen von Böhm-Bawerk[5] are the leading writers of the school. Their German forerunners are chronicled by Böhm-Bawerk, as are their English by Jevons; but, till Jevons and Menger, the doctrines now to be described were hardly before the public in either country.

Jevons seems to have had priority in time, having given his views to the British Association in 1862.[6] His complete exposition, however, first appeared with his *Political Economy* in 1871; and in that same year Menger published his *Grundsätze der Volkswirthschaftslehre*, in which he expounded the doctrine of value as Jevons had expounded it.

---

[1] Originally published in *The Quarterly Journal of Economics*, October 1888. James Bonar (1852–1941), British, was an historian of economic thought.

[2] *Political Economy*, Book III. Chap. 1, § 1.

[3] *Grundsätze der Volkswirtschaftslehre*. 299 pp. Vienna, 1871. English translation, *Principles of Economics* (Glencoe, Ill., Free Press of Glencoe, 1950; Grove City, Pa.: Libertarian Press, 1994, 328 pp.).

[4] *Ursprung und Hauptgesetze des wirthschaftlichen Werthes*. 228 pp. Vienna, 1884.

[5] Two papers in the *Jahrbücher für Nationalökonomie*, entitled *Grundzüge der Theorie des wirthschaftlichen Güterwerthes*: Part I, *Die Theorie des subjektiven Werthes*, in Vol. XIII, N.F. (1886); p. 1; Part II, *Die Theorie des objektiven Werthes, ibid.*, p.477. Reprinted in London School of Economics and Political Science Series of Reprints of Scarce Tracts in Economics and Political Science (London: The School, 1932).

[6] His paper is printed in the *Journal of the Statistical Society*, June, 1866, p. 282.

The Austrian writer seems to have owed nothing to the English.[7] Internal evidence alone would show that they were quite unconscious of each other's works. Their starting-points and their emphases are quite different. Jevons is suffering from reaction against Ricardo and J. S. Mill; and he lays most stress on his "General Mathematical Theory of Political Economy," or, in other words, his application of mathematical formulæ to the Benthamite Utilitarianism, upon which Ricardian economics had been largely founded.

Menger, on the other hand, is making stand against a very different enemy, the German Historical school, whose methods had departed only too far from Ricardo; and he recurs to a deductive method based (as Ricardo's professed to be) on known principles of nature and human nature, while following an apparently new path. He and his followers may occasionally make use of mathematical illustrations, but the important point with them is always what we may call (*pace* [thanks to] Böhm-Bawerk) the psychological analysis, which is distinctive, of their doctrine of value. Menger's somewhat heated controversy with Schmoller on the methodology of economics need not occupy us here, though it serves to throw light on the mental attitude which led him to his new economical starting-point.[8]

Turning now to Menger's *Principles of Economics*, we find him at the outset assigning to economics the investigation of certain principles, fixed independently of individual will, which determine what makes a thing "useful," a "good," and a thing "valuable" to me, and under what conditions an economical "exchange" of goods can take place, as well as under what conditions prices move up and down. Ricardo might possibly have used the same language, but his difference from Menger appears as soon as the principles are examined in detail.

Ricardo has given a theory of value that concerns only commercial values. Like Adam Smith, he identifies "value in use" with utility; and, though he describes it as absolutely essential to "value in exchange," he treats it as a mere preliminary *conditio sine qua non* [necessary condition], which explains no distinctive feature of value in exchange. The specific cause of value is regarded as one of two alternatives:[9] it is either the scarcity of the article in question or the quantity of labor required to obtain it. There are articles, he says, whose value is derived from scarcity alone, and which have "a value wholly independent of the

---

[7] Of his followers, Wieser shows most signs of assiduous study of Jevons.

[8] Compare *Quarterly Journal of Economics* for July, 1887, pp. 503, 504; *Jahrbücher für Nationalökonomie*, viii., N. F. (1884), p. 107 *et seq.*

[9] His illustrations show that he means one of two alternatives, and not a combination of two elements.

quantity of labor originally necessary to produce them and varying with the wealth and inclinations of those who are desirous to possess them."[10] He dismisses this kind of value as curtly as he dismissed value in use, and confines his inquiries to the exchange value of such goods as can be multiplied by labor or, to use a common phrase, are "freely produced."

To Menger and his followers, nearly every step in this proceeding is unsatisfactory. In the first place, they deny[11] that value in use is convertible with utility. They contend that the two are related as actuality to possibility. Utility means that an article is a possible cause of the satisfaction of my want; value, that it is the indispensable condition on which that satisfaction actually depends. All water and food are useful to a man; but, where both are present in abundance, they have no value for him, not even value in use: it is only when the satisfaction of his hunger *depends* on a particular loaf that that loaf will have value for him. The ordinary symptoms are that in the former case he is willing to waste, but not in the latter. In fact, utility and scarcity, the conjoint conditions of value in exchange in the case of *one* of Ricardo's two species of that phenomenon, are conjoint conditions of that value in use which is antecedent to both of them. Value to me means "importance for my welfare";[12] and a thing has no importance for my welfare if, in the first place, it can satisfy no want, and if, in the second, it exists with others like it in such abundance that I cannot consider myself absolutely dependent on it alone for my satisfaction, having all its fellows to serve my turn.

Differing thus at the outset from Ricardo's view of value in use, the Austrian economists take a different view of its place in economical investigation. They believe that, if Ricardo had paid due attention to value in use, or, as they variously call it, "subjective value," or "personal value,"[13] he would not have found his treatment of value in exchange encumbered with so many difficulties, and he need not have banished scarcity value to the limbo of economical anomalies.

As Jevons, in opposition to Mill, insists that the whole theory of Political Economy must depend on a correct theory of consumption, so

---

[10] *Political Economy and Taxation,* Chap.1.

[11] With Schäffle, in the treatise quoted below, *Ethische Seite,* p. 10.

[12] "Bedeutung," a phrase made current in this connection by Schäffle, the critic, as well as, in a sense, the forerunner of the Austrian school. See, *e.g.,* his *Ethische Seite der nationalökonomischen Lehre vom Werthe,* Tübingen, 1862. Compare his *Mensch und Gut,* 1861.

[13] "Subjective" value is a phrase of Neumann's adopted by Böhm-Bawerk. Wieser prefers "personal."

the writers of this school contend that the whole theory of value in exchange depends on a correct theory of value in use. "A national economics that leaves out the theory of subjective value is built on air."[14] One of them, indeed (Wieser), confines his main work entirely to this form of value.

Let us look at the manner in which they rear the building on this foundation. The difference, they say, between goods, or utilities, and economical goods, or values in use, being the difference between mere power to serve us and actual indispensableness to our service, is clearly a question of quantity. How, then, do we explain the paradox that such indispensable things as air and water have usually no value? The answer is that, though indispensable as a total, they are so unlimited in quantity that, in normal circumstances, no particular sample of them has any importance for our welfare. We must avoid the *fallacia sensus compositi et divisi.* Each part by itself is not indispensable. On the other hand, if we decrease the largeness of the whole, we bring the parts nearer and nearer to value till they actually reach it. We must, in all cases, regard ourselves as dealing with concrete wants and quantities, and not with generic or abstract; and we must in each given case be certain what our concrete facts are supposed to be. To a miller, a glass of water from his mill-stream has no value; for, if he has one dashed from his lips, he can get others from the same quarter. But let his total mill-stream be the concrete quantity considered, his total mill-stream has a great value to him, as he quickly shows, if his neighbor tries to cut it off from him. Yet, if mill-streams were as plentiful to him for working his mill as glassfuls of water from his own mill-stream are for quenching his thirst, he would attach as little value to the one as to the other. So air to a diver is to be had in limited quantities, and has value. To the ordinary man, air is to be had in unlimited quantities; and the particular quantity of it which he breathes is not indispensable, for he can get others like it, and it has therefore no value. In other words, the considerations applied by Ricardians to one case of value in exchange can be shown to apply to every case of value in use.

In the next place, still confining ourselves to value in use, we ask ourselves what are the degrees of value, and why one thing is recognized as more important to my welfare than another. The psychologists may settle why it is that men identify their interests with material things, and associate the satisfaction of a want, which is the real aim, with the material goods or outward acts, which are only the means of its satisfaction. The economist assumes the fact of identification, and

---

[14] Böhm-Bawerk.

considers the various forms it may take. In doing so, he meets with *contradictions économiques* similar to the one about air and water, and recurring in economical textbooks with the same tedious frequency as Caesar and Caius in formal logic.

Supposing that diamonds and loaves of bread are both important to my welfare, inasmuch as both of them satisfy my wants. Are not the two wants very different in kind, and is not the latter so much more important than the former that the loaves have a higher value in use than the diamonds, although the diamonds have the greater value in exchange? Without dealing with exchange at all at this stage, we can answer (1) that the loaves have not really, except in an absolute dearth, so great a value in use as the diamonds. And yet (2), of the two wants concerned with these two several objects, the want of food is undoubtedly more vital than the want of jewelry. We have therefore to consider in each case not only whether an article is or is not indispensable to the satisfaction of a want, but whether the want in question is high or low in our own particular scale of wants. For every man arranges his wants consciously or unconsciously in a certain scale of importance, and decides that some must be satisfied before others. Not only so, but he also arranges what Jevons would call the "increments" of the satisfaction of each of them in another scale, and judges that the first draught of satisfaction of the highest order of wants must come before any satisfaction of lower orders, while, at the same time, the lower orders may have a claim above the latest increments of the satisfaction of the higher. Food may be prized more highly than tobacco; but the latter may be prized more highly than a fourth meal in the day, pleasant, but not needful for health and energy, and not so pleasant as the pipe. Most wants are satisfied piecemeal, and there is always a point where satisfaction ceases and satiety supervenes. Hence, the scale of degrees acts in combination with the scale of kinds of wants; and both of them are influenced by the individual character and standard of living and aim in life, as well as by general laws of human nature. The two scales may be represented in a diagram (see below), which is taken with some slight alterations from Menger and Böhm-Bawerk,[15] and can be adapted and amplified at will by the reader.

If the "subject" concerned in the table were forced to retrench, he would encroach on the lowest lines of the latest columns first, or else the table has been inaccurate. As he was more closely pressed, he would ascend from right to left, till, if he were in desperate straits, all would go rather than the supply of the first degree of Want I.

---

[15] See, *e.g.*, *Jahrbücher*, xiii, N.F., p. 25. *Cf.* Jevons' *Political Economy*, Chap.3.

Degree	I. Food	II. Clothing	III. Lodging	IV. Smoking
First,	Necessary for life.			
Second,	Necessary for health.	First suit, necessary.		
Third,	Agreeable.	Second suit, convenient.	1 room.	
Fourth,	Less keenly agreeable.	Third suit, desirable.	2 rooms.	4 pipes a day.
Fifth,	Still, less keenly agreeable	Fourth suit, not unacceptable.	3 rooms.	8 pipes a day.
Sixth,	Satiety.	Fifth suit, satiety.	4 rooms, satiety.	Satiety.

The arithmetic of the table would not bear to be pressed. The difference in degree of importance between one meal when it is the only accessible one and one meal when it is *any* one of five alternate meals is not as 5 to 1, but as infinity to 1. When we draw near to absolute necessity, the increase in importance, as has been noticed by economical observers from Gregory King down, is geometrical rather than arithmetical. Even in the case of what is not a physiological or even a social necessary of life, but is only made a necessary by the conception which a particular individual has formed of ends of his own particular life, the importance of the object often increases with the decrease in its quantity in far greater than arithmetical proportion. The importance of a single available specimen of a particular Greek coin will to a collector be far more than double the importance of two specimens.

We become conscious of the gradations of our own scale of wants most clearly when we are either adding to our stock of goods or losing part of it, for an addition or subtraction might possibly affect the whole scale of wants, and would certainly affect parts of it. Looking further at our proceedings on such an occasion, we find that most of our stock of goods can be used to satisfy more than one kind of want. We may use corn for our own food, or we may feed our horses with it, or make spirits from it. How are we to judge what is the importance, or, in other words, the value, that is attached to an article having these alternative uses? The answer is—and it brings us to the central point of the theory: We judge of the value a man attaches to an article by the *lowest* use to which he is willing to put it. If he would light the fire with mahogany wood, the mahogany to him has simply a fire-lighting value. Or, if he would feed horses with his corn, he values corn at its horse-feeding value. He feeds himself with it, too, but he has enough of it to make any particular quantity of it only of the horse-feeding degree of importance to him. We judge that such and such a use is the *lowest* from the fact that, when the stock of goods is decreased, that use is first forgone. For example, if the supply of corn were cut short, the horses would lose first, or to take the other case the mahogany would cease to be used as firewood. The value of an article, therefore, is to be judged in every case by the importance of the least important want that a man would actually satisfy by means of the said article, for only to that want, and not to the others, is that article an indispensable condition of satisfaction. "Subjective value" depends not on utility, but on "final utility" *(Grenznutzen)* [marginal utility]—the lowest or least of the actual utilities rendered to us by the valuable article.

The theorists with whom we are dealing explain—one of them, Böhm-Bawerk, with peculiar care—that the "dependence" is not to be taken as a fact of causation, but as an ascertained fact of interpretation. Looking on any completed act of valuation, we find that, consciously or unconsciously, it involves this regard to the final utility. On the other hand, when the action of an economic agent is viewed, not as completed, but as still in prospect, it is not the minimum, but the maximum, of utility that we suppose to be kept in view by him. The act completed, however, we ask, What is his actually lowest maximum? And that is the final utility now under consideration.

Cases of daily life at once occur to the mind which this simple theory seems to leave unexplained. Böhm-Bawerk, whose skill in economical casuistry[16] is well known to readers of his book on *Theories of Interest*,[17] makes a brave attempt to clear up the difficulties. First of all, he says, we must not suppose the doctrine to mean that the final utility of a given whole is determined by the utility of its least useful part.[18] The value of the *whole* as a whole is determined by the final utility of the *whole*, and the value of the *parts* as such (i.e., not as conjoined, but as separate and alternative pluralities) is determined by the final utility of the *parts* as such. For example, if we ask ourselves what is the value of a skin of water in the desert to a traveller there, whose whole water supply it is, the answer is that the final utility of the whole skin—all or nothing—may be infinite. It may mean life or death to the man. He would not sacrifice it for any consideration. But consider it not as one and indivisible, but as a collection of separate cupfuls of water, then the value of each cupful as such is determined by, which means is judged from, the worst use to which the traveller is ever willing to put a cupful. If this be washing, then the value of each part is washing value,

---

[16] His own phrase.

[17] *Kapital und Kapitalzins.* Band I., *Geschichte und Kritik der Kapitalzins-Theorien.* 510 pp., Innsbrück, 1884. English translation, *Capital and Interest.* Volume I, *History and Critique of Interest Theories,* 490 pp. (S. Holland, Ill.: Libertarian Press, 1959).

[18] An interpretation countenanced by the language of Wieser and Jevons.

whereas the value of the whole as a whole is not washing value, but life or death value. In the second place, we are told that, though the final utility of the parts does not determine the value of the whole, yet it is rarely the case with any particular part that its value is settled by its own final utility. Or else we should judge the cupful that quenched thirst in the desert to be infinitely more valuable than the cupful that washed hands or clothes. In all the parts but one, the final utility that fixes their value for them is "an alien utility"—the final utility, not of themselves, but of some other part, which in the above instance is the washing cupful. In the third place, what is true of simpler specimens of the same kind of goods (e.g., cupfuls of water) is true of goods that are replaceable at the sacrifice of a substitute of a different kind, whether in the way of exchange or in a more direct way. The final utility determining its value is in that case again "an alien utility"—the utility of the worst used substitute. If I lose my coat and do not replace it, then its final utility has been also its total utility, its worst use was also its best. But, if I replace the lost coat by giving up something else to purchase a new one or to wear *as* a coat, then the coat's value was not its total, but its final utility, and the latter itself is not its own, but the final utility of the means of replacement, money or otherwise.

So far as we have followed our authors, we should infer that final utility was an analysis of the nature rather than of the causes of value. It states the fact itself rather than the reason for the fact. From their own description, value appears as the effect of two causes—utility and scarcity. The value of a shilling to me depends on its final utility in the sense that you only know its value to me if you know its final utility to me. In other words, its value *means* its final utility. There still remains the question—*why* its final utility is no more and no less, *why* I would use the shilling for what turns out to be the lowest purpose for which I would ever use it, *why* do I stop so soon, and not go to a lower purpose, or *why* do I not stop sooner, and not go so low? The answer is that the limit is fixed for me by my wants and my resources, taken together and in relation to each other; in other words, by the thing's utility and, in relation to my resources, its scarcity. My shillings are so comparatively abundant that I can satisfy my wants thus far and no farther by means of them. The circumstances of modern industrial society, it is true, introduce complications into these relations. The scarcity of an article in relation to me is determined not only by the extent of my resources, but by the resources and "effective demand" of other people, by the "supply and demand"[19] of the goods in question over society at large. In

---

[19] Expressions that are explained below.

ordinary cases, the said "supply and demand" affect the prices of goods, and therefore the extent of the deduction to be made from the individual's own store, when he replaces a lost article by a substitute. On the other hand, the Austrian writers justly contend, if it were not for the varying "scales" of wants and the correspondingly varying "subjective" values attached by different people to the same article, exchanges would not take place, and prices would not be settled as they are now. "Objective value in exchange" is the resultant of separate subjective valuations of the competing individuals in a commercial society.

It may confidently be said that, unless the doctrine of "subjective" value is made to throw light on value in exchange, economists would not care to linger over it as, after all, it is the social relations of human beings in the present industrial system that are of deepest interest to students of economics. Wieser's book, on its first appearance, was severely handled by Dietzel,[20] because the author did not show the application of his theory to the world with which ordinary economists had always dealt. Professor Böhm-Bawerk has, with great courage and ability, endeavored to remove this reproach from the school to which he belongs and his treatise on objective value must be almost our sole guide in the following exposition.

"Objective value," as he defines it, is by no means identical with value in exchange. Indeed, the latter becomes, from one point of view, a case of subjective and not of objective value. We may regard it as the importance to my welfare of an article exchanged by me instead of consumed by me. This close contact of "objective" with "subjective" value need not surprise anyone who remembers the general impossibility of keeping these two philosophical notions, subjectivity and objectivity, out of each other's reach. But for economical purposes, objective and subjective values may be kept apart without much practical difficulty. Objective value, according to our author, is best defined as simply the power of a commodity, considered out of relation to any particular subject, to produce certain effects. Firewood has heating value, food nourishing value and, if the particular power conferred is power to exchange for other articles, a commodity may have purchasing value. The said purchasing value or purchasing power is therefore only one species out of many belonging to the genus *objective value*. It is economically the most important, and is practically the only one discussed by Böhm-Bawerk under this head.[21] He rightly refuses to confine the term

---

[20] See *Jahrbücher*, xi., N. F. (1885), p. 161.

[21] Others are, *e.g.*, letting value, hiring value, productive value (productiveness).

"value" to one of the two main kinds, objective and subjective, or to attempt to prove that the two are forms of one and the same kind of value. He accepts both senses, because both are deeply rooted in the common language of men. And he tries to avoid ambiguity by means of the distinctive philosophical epithets, subjective and objective. It seems on the whole, as precise a distinction as can usually be procured in economics though, to English readers at least, the terminology would be a serious stumbling-block.

Value in exchange being first defined as the power one thing has to fetch others in exchange, the next preliminary definition is that of *price*, which is said to be not "value expressed in money" but the actual equivalent goods, whether money or not, given in exchange. The *value* in exchange of a coat is thus its power to exchange, say, for two pairs of boots or for £4 in money. The *price* of the coat is, then, the two pairs of boots or the £4 in money. The distinction, it may be admitted, is intelligible, and can be preserved with a very fair amount of consistency. We are, however, at once led by it face to face with the familiar question of economical textbooks. How is the price itself explained? The answer is that under free competition of buyers and sellers and on the supposition that each of them is seeking his own greatest immediate advantage, the price is determined by the subjective value of the article concerned to the least strong[22] of the actual sellers and the least strong of the actual buyers. The case is analogous to that of subjective value where the criterion, too, is not the worst of all possible, but the worst of all actual uses. A strong seller, again, is one who attaches comparatively little value to his article, and can therefore come a long way down or let it go for comparatively little. A strong buyer is one who attaches much value to the article he would buy and can therefore go a long way up or give a great deal for it. And the least strong of the actual sellers and the least strong of the actual buyers determine the selling price.

The normal case may be illustrated by the subjoined diagram[23] where the articles offered are horses, all supposed of the same quality. There are only five pairs that can exchange at all with economical advantage and these are the five strongest buyers and sellers. The price is determined by the valuations of the least strong of these; namely, A^5 and B^5. B^5 can take anything over £40. A^5 can give anything under £44. The price will be between the two figures.

---

[22] *Tauschfähigkeit*—strength in exchanging—a notion first fully treated by Menger, is much used by Böhm-Bawerk.

[23] *Cf.* Böhm-Bawerk, *Jahrbücher*, xiii., N. F., p. 495.

WOULD-BE BUYERS. (Subjectively)			WOULD-BE SELLERS. (Subjectively)		
A^2	Values a horse at	£60	B^1	Values a horse at	£20
A^2	" "	56	B^2	" "	22
A^3	" "	52	B^3	" "	30
A^4	" "	48	B^4	" "	34
A^5	" "	44	B^5	" "	40
A^6	" "	42	B^6	" "	43
A^7	" "	40	B^7	" "	50
A^8	" "	36	B^8	" "	52
A^9	" "	34			
A^{10}	" "	30			

An objection occurs. If the price is determined by the buyer's estimate of the article's value in use,[24] and if that, in the normal case of replacement by substitutes, depends on the buyer's estimate of the value in use to him of the means of replacement, does not this mean that the market price depends on the market price? The answer given by our author is as follows: When the buyer comes forward to get his substitute, he carries in his mind a presumption as to the state of the market. He values his coat at a certain lower figure, because he has a certain presumption as to the scarcity of coats. He has presumed that substitutes can always be got at that presumed figure. The said presumption has determined his use and abuse of his coat all along, and till he comes to the market it is perfectly rational. But in the market itself he must not presume. He must see for himself how the supply and demand actually stand, and raise or lower his estimate accordingly.

What, then, is the meaning of the "supply and demand"? These are terms for which Böhm-Bawerk has little respect, regarding them as the natural refuge of confused thinkers; but, since they are rooted in language, they must be explained. To explain them, he gives an account of the real reasons why the "subjective valuations" of what he calls the "terminal pair"[25] in the above diagram are at the height assigned. The said height is a result, *first* of the numbers of the would-be buyers, *second* of the degree of value these would-be buyers attach to the article concerned, *third* of the numbers of would-be sellers, and *fourth* of the degree of value they attach to the article they would sell. Again, in the

---

[24] It must be said, once for all, that Böhm-Bawerk dislikes this term; but it has been kept as the most familiar English equivalent for the *quasi*-philosophical "subjective value."

[25] *Grenzpaar*, on the analogy of *Grenznutzen*, which for its part may be translated either final or terminal utility, both terms used by Jevons.

"degree of value" so specified is involved a comparison between the article concerned and the other article (say money) which is to constitute the price of it. If a buyer is said to value a horse at £40, this means that one horse has more importance for his welfare than forty sovereigns. It is a comparison of the two, horse and money, that determines the maximum amount of his offer. And, as the same is true, *mutatis mutandis* [the necessary changes being made] of the seller, we must add to the above four reasons two more, the value of the *price* to the buyer and the value of the *price* to the seller.

But from the whole of this statement it is clear that two-thirds of the conditions of objective value depend on a comparison between wants and their means of satisfaction[26] over society as a whole. The old doctrine that "prices are regulated by the relation of supply and demand" was, we are told, not false if the terms were understood to include not only the number of articles offered and desired, but the various motives influencing the buyers and sellers respectively. It is when demand and supply are both taken as quantities and the price is said to depend on the suppliers and demanders agreeing to supply and demand the same quantity[27] that the formula is wrong, for the height of the price depends not on the *quantities* offered and demanded, but on the eagerness of the sellers and buyers. So, also, demand is often divided into effective and ineffective. But this is only right if it is remembered that "ineffectiveness" includes want of will as well as want of power. The demanders excluded from the fixing of the price are those who are not prepared to pay a certain price, either because "their poverty and not their will consents" to their withdrawal or because their notions of the subjective value of the article to them do not allow them to pay the price. Intensity of desire, too, can be recognized as a condition of a strong demand only if qualified in a similar way by the double limitation of resources and of standard living—in fact, if it is made as much a matter of will-ing as of wish-ing.

It is, however, in regard to supply that the most burning questions arise. Ricardo hardly allowed demand to influence price at all. When we ask on what depends the lowest figure at which the supplier is prepared to sell his ware, we are told by the supporters of the ordinary orthodox doctrine that—in addition to the value, for the seller, of the article he is selling, and the value, for the same seller, of the article, usually money, for which he is offering it—we must take into account the

---

[26] *Bedarf und Deckung.*

[27] Mill, Book III. Chap. 2 § 3: "The ratio intended is that between the quantity demanded and the quantity supplied." The next paragraph (§ 4) is in greater agreement with Böhm-Bawerk.

cost of production. But according to our authors the connection of cost with price is not to be found in any influence of the former on the decision of the supplier to sell or not to sell at a given minimum price. He will not sell for less than the article is *subjectively* worth to him. But he may and often does sell it below its cost, however reluctantly. The real connection between cost and price is the effect of cost on the *number* of articles produced. The law of cost is not to be opposed to the law of supply and demand, as if they were rivals on equal terms. Cost is only intelligible in relation to supply and demand, and in a very subordinate relation. The law of cost is a particular law of supply: it formulates the conditions of the supply, not of all articles, but of those that are "freely produced."

The discussion has reached a point where it has more than a mere academic interest, and no apology need be made for a somewhat full statement of the application of the doctrine of the Austrian school to the special questions of cost and the means of production. These questions come up first of all in writings before us under the head of *subjective value*, though they are most familiar in ordinary economical discussions in connection with exchange and distribution. We are told that, to get a clear view of the situation, we must follow Menger in arranging the means of production according to their nearness to their final products. Let us call these last goods of the "first rank"—say, the finished loaf—goods one step removed, goods of the "second rank" say, bread a-baking in the oven,—another step removed, goods of the "third rank"—the flour in the mill—and so on till we get to the farthest traceable ranks—the elements from which the crops in the field are derived. The instruments used in the various ranks are, we suppose, to be ranked according to their respective goods, though it is materials alone that are mentioned by our author. The water-wheel, as affecting goods of third rank—grain becoming flour—would be itself of third rank. The description given by Menger[28] of capital as "nothing but a total of complementary goods of higher rank," i.e., of a rank remote from the finished article, now becomes intelligible.[29] But, as to the question of cost, we want to know what determines (a) the subjective and (b) the exchange value of these remote means of production, whether instruments or materials. Now, on the principles of the school, the subjective

---

[28] See *Volkswirthschaftslehre*, pp. 127. seq. [*Principles of Economics*, pp. 152 ff.]. But in his article on "Capital" in the *Jahrbücher*, July 1888, Menger desires to confine the term Capital to "money devoted to increase of income," and to use "means of production," as the least ambiguous term, in such investigations as the one now before us.

[29] See Böhm-Bawerk's *Kapital und Kapitalzins*. I, pp. 6, 246, 247 [*Capital and Interest.* I, pp. 4, 130].

value of these must mean, as subjective value means in all other cases, that they are an indispensable condition of my satisfaction, and thereby have importance for my welfare. In their case, it is true, they are a condition of a condition, but the indirectness does not alter the fact. "Praedicatum praedicati praedicatum subjecti?"

Let the final product be called A, and its means of production G^2, G^3, G^4, in order of remoteness. Let us assume for simplicity that these means of production are concerned only with this one article, and have no collateral or by-products. On what does the subjective value of each member of the series depend? The value of the finished article (or A) is determined by its final utility. As to the article of the second rank (G^2), if it were absent, we should lose the finished article (A) itself, and with it its final utility. In other words, the want satisfied by A depends, not only on A, but on G^2; and, as G^2 depends on G^3, A depends on G^3, and for a like reason on G^4. In other words, all the successive and cooperating means of production, through all ranks of the series, are conditions of the final utility of their ultimate product, the article to be consumed. It follows (1) that the value of all members of the series is in principle one and the same, (2) that greatness or smallness of value is fixed, *in the last resort*, by the finished article's final utility, and (3) that it is fixed, *in the first instance*, for each member by the member directly succeeding it, or, in other words, produced by it. In practice, men do not refer to the last so much as to the first instance. They often take the former for granted on the strength of the commercial knowledge of themselves or others. A timber merchant, when he is considering what is the value to him of wood for cask staves, does not trouble himself about the ultimate destiny of the staves, but only about the quantity of them he can make out of a given quantity of wood, and for how much, when made, they will sell in the existing state of the market. Yet, if casks went out of use and fell in price, his staves would follow suit—the value of the means of production thus proving its dependence on the value of the finished product.

On the other hand, it will be said that, as a matter of experience, we find the value of goods rising or falling with their "cost." Now, the cost is nothing but the total of the "productive goods," labor, capital, and any other outlay which must be expended to furnish a certain product. On this, it is to be remarked that "identity of cost and value" is only another phrase for the identity of the value of the means of production with that of the product, without any invidious indication of precedence. Popular language, however, too often suggests that the value of the product is *determined by* the cost of production, whereas the truth (according to our authors) is that the value of the "cost-goods" is determined by the value of the product. Our authors differ both from the "labor theory," which refers all value to cost and all cost to labor, and from the "Dualistic"[30] or Ricardian theory, which alleges two distinct sources of value (usefulness and cost), and refers to the one whatever it cannot explain by the other. But, as the statement of a mere tendency or approximation, the doctrine that value is identical with cost is, they admit, substantially true in the case of freely produced articles, any discrepancies in their case between cost and value being occasioned by the fact that production takes time, and between the first step in production and the last result of it, men and things may have altered. The wants of men, the comparative quantities of goods in the market and men's views about them, may change; and then their estimate of the subjective value of the goods employed in production will change also. Such discrepancies are beyond any fixed rule. There is, however, another discrepancy, which is permanent and regular; and it is the discrepancy caused by the mere length of time taken in the conversion of the means of production into the finished product. The value of the means of production in the remote ranks will lag steadily behind the value of the finished product, in the proportion to the length of time taken in the passage from the former to the latter. In this kind of discrepancy, Böhm-Bawerk sees the real key to the phenomenon of interest on capital, though he has not as yet given his views to the public at length on this point. But, in the discussion of cost, he asks us to neglect both of the above kinds of discrepancy.

Let us now retract the assumption which we made,[31] that the given means of production concern only one kind of product. In most cases, the goods of second, third, or fourth rank, in the regress of the economic observer, may be capable of producing not one kind of article only, but a number of alternatives. Iron may be made into nails or ploughshares or fire-grates or fifty other things. The question to be asked is: Which of the alternative products determines the value of the common means of production?

Suppose a sample of G^2 to produce either A or B or C, and the final utility of A to be 100, of B 120, of C 200. The final utility of their common means of production, a sample of G^2, will be the lowest[32]—namely, 100, for if we had only two samples of G^2 and had therefore to lose one of

---

[30] Böhm-Bawerk, in *Jahrbücher*, xiii, N.F., p. 61.

[31] *Cf.* Menger, *Volkswirthschaftslehre*, pp. 40 to 45 [*Principles of Economics* pp. 84–89]. See above, p. 19.

[32] That is, will be *according* to the lowest, allowance being made for discrepancy of time and for the other cooperating elements— labor, etc. Böhm-Bawerk, *Jahrbücher*, xiii., N. F., p. 538.

the three—A, B, and C—it would be A, as the lowest, that would be sacrificed, and it is therefore *its* existence that depends on a third sample of G^2. Therefore, a G^2, when it can be economically used to produce A at all, is in value to us as A, and not as B or C. In the same way, it might be shown that, of several alternative uses of a G^3, the lowest, or that which leads to the lowest actually valued utility will determine the value of G^3. It appears, then, that the value of the least valuable ultimate product of those products economically produced at all determines the value of the antecedent means of production from the lowest rank to the highest.

We have next to ask what determines the value of the two other alternative products, B and C. If their own final utility is 120 and 200 respectively, then their value would be greater than that of their means of production, which has been shown to become 100. But, as a B or C, if lost, can be replaced by a substitute made from G^2 at the sacrifice of A, the said B and C will, by reasoning given in an earlier stage of this discussion, fall to the value of G^2; i.e., to 100 instead of 120 and 200. In fact, to our surprise, we find that, in the case of replaceable alternatives, it is, in all instances but one, the cost that determines the degree of value after all; and the common identification of cost and price is therefore, in their case only, perfectly justified.[33] It is an "alien" final utility that determines their value; and the alien utility in this case is that of an article which rules the value, also, of the cost-goods. Their value is therefore the same as that of their cost-goods. Though the road is roundabout, the point reached is the same as in the old Ricardian doctrine. Of freely producible goods, it is really as nearly true to say their cost determines their value as to say the west wind causes the rain.[34]

Let us now apply the doctrine to the value that "dwells not in particular will," namely to *objective value in exchange* and to *price* whether in money or in other goods. These last result, as we have seen, from the subjective valuations of the finished product by the consumers. And, in their turn, they determine the demand, which is confronted by the stocks of producers as the supply. The market selling price results from the competition of subjective valuers, as already described.

Now, in each case, the height of the market price determines the height of the *subjective* value in exchange, and the value of the least valuable of the actually sold products determines the subjective value of the means of production. Each producer will subjectively value his means of production—say, iron—according to the market price of the

---

[33] Compare above, pp. 18–19.

[34] Böhm-Bawerk, *Kapital und Kapitalzins,* I, p. 442 [*Capital and Interest,* I, p. 301].

article he makes out of it. One producer will value it, say, at 30s., another at 40s., another at 80s. a ton. With these valuations, they go to the market. The *extent* of their demand is in proportion to the expected sale of their own goods. The *intensity* of their demand is in proportion to their several valuations above mentioned. No one will give more than the price he hopes to get for his article. The extremes would be say, 2s. and 20s. The supply would be the stocks of iron from the mines, which will pass to the strongest buyers at a price between the estimate of the weakest of the said strongest and the estimate of the would-be buyer that just fails to be an actual buyer. The estimates in a great modern market would be so accurate that we may say the price is equal to the estimate of the lowest buyer. Now, as the lowest buyer's estimate depends on the price of his own article, the said article is the limiting article or *Grenzprodukt* [marginal product], the least valuable of the uses to which iron can, in given circumstances, be economically put at all. But for all goods above that lowest there is an inducement to makers to increase their supplies, and, the more this is done, the lower sinks the point where supply and demand balance each other, till at last, in the case of the next lowest sellers, the price goes down to the limiting point, where it ceases to be profitable. This is how all prices tend to be identical with cost in the case of freely producible goods.

Such is, in outline, the theory of the Austrian school. To readers not familiar with its by-paths, it suggests some obstinate questionings. Those discussions of the relation of wants and the subject of wants to the means of satisfaction seem too easily apt, unless confined within rigid limits, to convert economical discussion into psychological. Even Böhm-Bawerk, who considers that the line of demarcation can be easily drawn, does not in practice avoid a blending of psychology with economics. A utilitarian psychology and ethics have colored his whole theory, as they colored that of Jevons. He makes the possibility of the doctrine of final utility to depend on the commensurability of pains and pleasures. He makes the individual subject the sole judge of what is his final utility and of what to him, therefore, is "economical," or the opposite.[35] But this is very different from the hypothesis of the older economists, whose "economical man" was gifted with enlightened, as distinguished from unenlightened, self-interest. And it is remarkable that, as soon as the Austrian economist reaches their problem—objective value in exchange—he adopts their assumption, and tells us that his theory of exchanges is true of men who are pursuing their own gain with pru-

---

[35] Böhm-Bawerk, *Jahrbücher,* xiii, N. F., pp. 13, 50, etc. Yet he speaks, on page 55, of a "true" as distinguished from an apparent value.

dence and knowledge. There was surely no need to throw the "rays of utilitarian darkness" into the subject at all. Such a table of wants as is given above (page 16) might be drawn up by philosophers of widely different schools or by ordinary economists without any philosophy at all. To introduce the philosophical theory that all motives are pleasures or pains, and each individual is the supreme judge of his own ends, is to cast doubt on the existence of any objective truth in the whole matter and to make the very distinction between economy and waste an incomprehensible riddle. It may be added that, to those who believe that economic processes can and ought to be studied separately from philosophy, even though the economists' results need to be complemented and supplemented by the sublimer study, the very use of philosophical terms for economical facts seems unnecessary and inexpedient.

But, looking now at the general conclusions of the Austrian theorists, we may observe that they involve no "Copernican change of attitude" or, in other words, no complete revolution in economic doctrine. The seeds of the new views may be found in the old economists.[36] Not to go back to Lauderdale or Malthus, we find in such passages as the fifteenth chapter of Mill's Third Book, for example, a full acknowledgment of the important part played by "subjective value" in economical processes:

> If one thing [says Mill, speaking of the Measure of Value], either by itself or by what it would purchase, could maintain a laboring man for a day, and another could maintain him for a week, there would be some reason in saying that the one was worth, for ordinary human uses, seven times as much as the other. But this would not measure the worth of the thing to its possessor for his own purposes, which might be greater to any amount, though it could not be less, than the worth of the food which the thing would purchase.

And, in the passage immediately following this the well-known section on Joint Cost of Production, Mill distinctly speaks of the "law of supply and demand" as "a law anterior to cost of production and more fundamental ." In an earlier passage, he had said that "the utility of a thing in the estimation of a purchaser is the extreme limit of its exchange value." (Book III. chap. ii. § 1)

---

[36] Professor Böhm-Bawerk, (who has been kind enough to read the manuscript of the paper) points out that he has amply acknowledged this in his second paper on Value, *Jahrbücher,* xiii, N. F., p. 502).

The idea so common in economical writers, from Lauderdale[37] down to J. S. Mill, that "wealth" consists of "desirable things limited in quantity," gains its clearest interpretation when wealth is understood as a sum total of things subjectively valuable, in the sense defined by the Austrian school. Nothing but this will save such a saying as, "Though air is not wealth, mankind are much richer by obtaining it gratis," from self-contradiction.

The service, therefore, that Jevons and the Austrians have rendered to economic theory seems to be, not the first introduction into it of "subjective value," as if that were a new thing, but the clearer definition of it. "Final utility" is rather a definition of value than an explanation of its causes, and the charm of a new term, itself in need of explanation, seems to have led them to exaggerate its merits at the expense of more vital parts of their own doctrine. Even by their own accounts, the notion of "final utility" throws light rather on the nature than on the causes of value. And, as with wealth, so with value, the causes are our real difficulty. The service of the school is to have shown, not merely that "subjective value" means final utility, but that the causes of subjective value are the causes of all economic value whatever, whether value in use or value in exchange. Jevons himself makes practical acknowledgment of this when in his *Primer* (1878), he gives the causes of value in great detail but says nothing at all of "final utility."

Again it may be doubted whether the Austrian economists have fairly met the challenge made by their critics to show the application of their doctrine to the modern world of exchanges.[38] Böhm-Bawerk in his reply to Dietzel's review of Wieser's book[39] does not deny their obligation to do this and the whole of his second treatise on objective value may be considered an attempt to fulfill the obligation. At the same time, the criticisms passed by him, by Menger, and by Wieser on such views as the "cost theory," and especially the "labor theory" of value, masterly as they often are, are upon the whole such as might have been used by economists like Wagner or Cohn, who differ from them on what they treat as the main question. Those are signs that the shrewdest of the socialists themselves are ceasing to stake their political and social plans on the too vulnerable theories of Robertus and Marx, and that they would hardly dispute this part of the ground any longer. In any case, such propositions as that of Jevons, that "labor once spent has no

---

[37] On *Public Wealth*, p. 57.

[38] Emil Sax has applied it to taxation in his *Grundlegung der theoretischen Staatswirthschaft*. See *Quarterly Journal of Economics*, July 1887, p. 504.

[39] "Theory of Subjective Value," *Jahrbücher*, xiii, N.F., p. 77, seq. For Dietzel's review, see *Jahrbücher*, xi, pp. 161, 162.

influence on the future value of any article," are so far from peculiar to the school that, as Wieser points out, they might be deduced from the reasonings of Mill himself.[40] The very idea of final utility might perhaps have been suggested by Ricardian doctrine that rent is determined by the fertility of the least fertile soil in profitable cultivation, and we might speak of the Ricardian law of rent as the principle of *final fertility*. Its affinity with final utility has, in fact, saved the doctrine of rent from alteration at the hands of Jevons or the Austrian economists.

In regard to the doctrine of capital, interest, profits, and wages, Böhm-Bawerk has followed Menger's view of capital, as above mentioned, rather than the narrower view of Jevons, who confines it exclusively to means of maintaining laborers. The relation of labor, wages, and profits to value is treated incidentally in Böhm-Bawerk's *History and Critique of Interest Theories*. In the second paper on value, we are expressly told[41] that, in the analysis there given, abstraction has been made of labor, tools, and industrial processes. The case, in fact, has been presented abstractly or under simplified conditions, and, if we are to see the whole truth about objective value in exchange, we must recur to the views expressed by the author in the larger work.[42] There we are told that the amount and duration of the capital advanced, as distinguished from the labor bestowed, in production prevent value from any exact coincidence with cost in any case whatsoever. Ricardo's qualifications of his "labor theory" are described as of undoubted truth and importance. Ricardo rightly saw that the proportions in which fixed and circulating capital enter into cost will seriously affect value in exchange. Now, it would strengthen the position of Professor Böhm-Bawerk and his colleagues very considerably if he would explain, not critically, but positively, the precise effect of these and other modifications on his own theory of value in exchange. We should like to know, for example, what the value of labor is, when considered as a question of the objective value of services, which our author expressly allows to be "goods,"[43] and, therefore, to be constituents in a complementary group of means of production. Does cost in wages play the same secondary part in objective value in exchange as cost in material goods?

---

[40] Wieser, pp. 113, 114; Mill, Book II, chap. xvi, § 5. Cf. what is said of von Thünen's doctrine of rent by Böhm-Bawerk, *Jahrbücher*, xiii, p. 505.

[41] *Jahrbücher*, xiii, p. 538, n.

[42] *Kapital und Kapitalzins*, I, pp. 401–407. [English translation, *Capital and Interest*, I, pp. 162–167; 287- 290.]

[43] *Rechte und Verhältnisse vom Standpunkte der volkswirthschaftlichen Güterlehre*, pp. 158. Innsbrück, 1881. See pp. 31, 57, 61. [English translation "Whether Legal Rights and Relationships are Economic Goods" in *Shorter Classics of Eugen von Böhm-Bawerk* (South Holland, Ill.: Libertarian Press, 1962)].

Would he subscribe to the doctrine of Jevons and Walker that wages are a residuum remaining after deduction of certain fixed elements and depending essentially, therefore, on the amount of the produce? Would he regard profits as a fixed element at all or, when distinguished from interest and "wages of superintendence," as entering into cost at all?

The only writer of the school who has gone at any length into the above difficulties is Professor Emil Sax, of Prague, whose book on the economics of the State[44] includes an account of general economic principles. His views, in the main, are those of Böhm-Bawerk, but he will not allow that "services" are goods, or that labor is a service. When we say that "wages" are paid, we mean, according to Sax, simply that the capitalist purchases the workman's part of the product while the product is still a-making.[45] Labor is not a commodity. Neither are wages "a recompense for the services of the workman." They are "the price of the workman's share of the commodity produced; it is his own product that constitutes his wages." Contract-wages depend on a calculation, made in advance, of the probable price of the product. "Cost of production" means the value of the total of capitalized goods expended in the production, as compared with the value of the product itself when finished. Without value, objective market value in exchange, there would be no trustworthy means of comparing present sacrifice and future returns or, if you like, past sacrifice and present returns.[46] The employer, therefore, thinks entirely of the market price which he is likely to get for his finished article. The subjective value to himself of the said article does not come into the calculation and hence it is that, roughly speaking, like work has like wages. It is otherwise with "services"—e.g., of professional men—where the subjective value to the person served is almost the ruling element in the price and the payments are therefore very various.[47] There, too, the payments are made by the served to the server in goods made by the labor of the served or of his workmen. But, in hired labor for wages, the worker really receives not another's, but his own product in the garb of its price.[48]

The relation of employer and employed is due to the institution of property, enabling me as it does to turn even the objects of immediate consumption, such as food, into means of procuring new goods: it

---

[44] *Grundlegung der theoretischen Staatswirthschaft*, Vienna, 1887, which should be read in conjunction with the author's *Wesen und Aufgaben der Nationalökonomik*, 1884. For the general drift, see *Quarterly Journal of Economics*, July 1887, p. 504.

[45] *Staatswirthschaft*, p. 230, note; cf. 242, 247, 322, 333.

[46] *Ibid.*, pp. 328, 330.

[47] *Ibid.*, 242.

[48] *Staatswirthschaft*, 246, 247, note; cf. 242.

embraces in this way "acquisition" by means of the production of others, in addition to "production" of my own. There are persons, for example, who want the food, but have no goods at the moment to give for it in exchange. Accordingly, I give them the food on condition that at some future time they shall make and hand over to me other goods for the satisfaction of my future wants. Self-interest demands that the amount of the required future equivalent shall be at least great enough to balance the comparatively greater, subjective, value of the food as a present, in contrast with a future, means of satisfaction. Capital, therefore, besides becoming the means of production, may without losing its nature be devoted to the present satisfaction of present wants, that is, the present wants of others who will then produce for my future benefit. "Means of production" should, strictly speaking, apply only to the capital laid out otherwise than in wages; but the extension of the phrase to the latter case is justifiable for, if I get two sacks of corn a year for every one sack that I have given in wages, it is just as if I had myself used one for seed and reaped two at the harvest. As a rule, the workmen having little or no property are obliged to purchase the means of living by selling me in advance their share of the product. Their dependent situation is due, like payment of interest on capital, to the existence of private property.[49]

Professor Sax does not enter into the further details of distribution. He refers, in the manner of ordinary economists, to the competition of workmen with each other and to their standard of living as affecting the amount of their share in the product and, in the manner of the socialism which he disclaims, to "the necessary labor" as an item in the calculations about any production.[50] But, like his leader Menger, he bids us look for further light to the forthcoming work of the Innsbrück professor, Böhm-Bawerk. Böhm-Bawerk is, therefore, at the present moment the foremost champion of the Austrian school of economics. To procure a favorable hearing, the school must apply its principles without reserve to the problems of distribution as they meet us in modern countries. This is one of the services for which we look to the long promised second volume on *Interest Theories*.

---

[49] *Ibid.*, pp. 322–323.
[50] *Staatswirthschaft*, pp. 334, 335.

Economics at Berlin and Vienna[1]

by H. R. Seager

Since the publication of Roscher's *Grundriss zu Vorlesungen über die Staatswissenschaften nach geschichtlicher Methode* in 1843, in which the ideas, since characterized as those of the Historical school, first found systematic formulation, Germany has been the scene of an almost uninterrupted struggle for supremacy between conflicting opinions concerning the most fundamental questions in political economy. Among these questions there is none more interesting or more vital than that as to the proper method to be employed in economic investigations, and few intellectual battles have been fought with more vigor and with a more equal mustering of ability in the rival camps than has the famous *Methodenstreit* [struggle over methods]. For some time it seemed as if the Historical school was going to carry all before it. Its acute criticisms of the system of economics built up, largely with the aid of abstraction and deduction by Adam Smith and his immediate followers, were unanswerable. Attacked also by the Socialists, economic theory was rapidly falling into ill repute, and with it the method upon which it had rested.

As was to be expected, a reaction set in. The leader in this reaction was Professor Carl Menger, of Vienna; who, in his *Grundsätze der Volkswirtschaftslehre*, published in 1871, tried to demonstrate, that the errors of the Classical school were due not to the choice of a wrong method but to the wrong use of a right method, by employing the same method of abstraction and deduction to arrive at theories more in harmony with observed facts. In 1883, attacking the methodological question directly, he published his *Untersuchungen über die Methode der Socialwissenschaften, und der Politischen Ökonomie insbesondere*,[2] in which he subjected the doctrines of the Historical school to a thorough-going criticism. He concluded that for theoretical economics there is but one method—that which he calls the *"exact"* method, founded, to be sure, upon an analysis of the materials furnished by economic history and by

---

[1] Originally published in *Journal of Political Economy*, March 1893. Henry Rogers Seager (1870–1930), economist, taught at Columbia University, 1902–1930.

[2] English translation: *Problems in Economics and Sociology* (Urbana, Ill.: University of Illinois Press, 1963); reprinted as *Investigation into the Method of the Social Sciences, with Special Reference to Economics* (New York: New York University Press, 1985; Grove City, Pa.: Libertarian Press, 1996).

everyday experience, and requiring to be verified by observation, but quite distinct from the inductive method.

Of all the criticisms called forth by this work none was more uncompromising than that of Professor Gustav Schmoller, of Berlin. In the polemic which followed, Professor Schmoller figured as the leader of the extreme left of the Historical school, and would hear nothing of economic theory in the present unripe condition of our science. Professor Menger, on the other hand, asserted that, without theory, economic science, as all science, is impossible. The controversy was heated and of an unnecessarily personal character, and without doubt both parties to it said rather more than they intended. It was nonetheless of a decided scientific value and did much to clear the atmosphere of many misapprehensions concerning the real nature of the methodological question that were common to both. If this question was not thereby finally settled it was, at any rate, placed in a clearer light.

What Professor [Alfred] Marshall says in regard to method may be quoted as a very fair summing up of contemporary German opinion: "Induction and deduction go hand in hand. . . .There is not any one method of investigation which can properly be called the method of economics; but every method must be made serviceable in its proper place."[3] To some minds this denotes that the question of method is really a question of temperament and intellectual bent. Let everyone employ that method that seems best fitted to his hand; the field is large enough for all, working with all sorts of tools. To others such a glossing over of the question is decidedly unsatisfactory. To them such an answer points eloquently to the backward condition of economic science, and calls, not for indifference respecting the question of method, but for a more strict classification of the economic sciences. If there is room for the employment of all methods in political economy, it is high time we were deciding what particular method is appropriate to each particular department of the subject.

It is a partial answer to this question—a very concise one, unfortunately—which Professor Menger has attempted to give in his latest writing upon this subject.[4] There remains to be written, however, a comprehensive summing up of the whole question, a logic from the standpoint of the economic sciences, and it is upon such a work that Professor Menger is now engaged.

Not only because of the prominent part they have taken in the

---

[3] *Principles of Economics*, 2d ed., pp. 88 and 89.

[4] *Grundzüge einer Klassification der Wirtschaftswissenschaften*. Conrad's *Jahrbücher*, n. 7, Bd. xix, pp. 1–32.

methodological controversy, but also because of their contributions to economic literature in other fields, on the one hand to economic theory and on the other to economic history and statistics, Professors Carl Menger and Gustav Schmoller are today two of the most conspicuous figures in the German economic world of letters.

While the war of methods has been waging between the Menger faction and the Schmoller faction of German economists, Professor Adolph Wagner, the distinguished colleague of Professor Schmoller, at Berlin, has been devoting his prodigious energy to working out his own scientific ideas in his own way. Today he is conspicuous as the acknowledged German authority on all questions of public finance, and as the editor and, to a large extent, the writer, of a handbook on political economy[5] which, for comprehensiveness, promises to be an advance upon the well-known, three-volume handbook edited by Professor Schönberg.

At Vienna, working along by the side of, and in fruitful cooperation with, Professor Menger, is Professor Eugen von Böhm-Bawerk. At present actively employed in helping to bring order out of the chaos of Austrian finances, he yet finds time to conduct a seminar, and to meet students really interested in economic questions, at his very pleasant home. Professor Böhm-Bawerk has been called the *"Ricardo* of the Austrian School," of which, by a less apt comparison, Professor Menger is the *Adam Smith*. Böhm-Bawerk has certainly won for himself a lasting place in the history of the development of economic thought by his two-volume work *Capital and Interest,* be his conclusions accepted as final or not,[6]

To these four men, Menger, Schmoller, Böhm-Bawerk, and Wagner, the eyes of the economists of all nations are at present directed, as to the most conspicuous representatives of our science in the country in which that science has been most assiduously and most fruitfully cultivated during the last fifty years. To the great universities, which are the scenes of their pedagogic activities, attaches an unusual interest for economists. Berlin and Vienna are at the present time magnets, attracting to themselves economic students from all countries. A description of the work being done in political economy at these institutions would, therefore, seem not out of place in the *Journal of Political Economy. . . .*

---

[5] The handbook is divided into five principal parts, and will consist of at least fourteen volumes. *Cf.* Wagner, *Grundlagen der Volkswirtschaft.* Leipzig, 1892, pp. 2 and 3.

[6] There are at present three rival theories in the field, all based upon the marginal utility theory of value, viz.: the theories advanced respectively by Professors Böhm-Bawerk, Menger and Wieser.

University of Berlin:

Professors Wagner and Schmoller, though differing decidedly in their convictions concerning many of the most fundamental questions of the science, have, nevertheless, for some years worked along side by side in outward harmony. Those students for whom questions of theory and of public finance have a special interest usually count themselves Wagner's pupils; others with a bent for historical and statistical researches fall as naturally to Schmoller. . . .

Professor Adolph Wagner, although already in his fifty-eighth year, retains unimpaired the energy and enthusiasm of a young man. Beginning his economic career as the pupil and follower of Rau, he gradually outgrew the ideas of the Classical school, was in 1872 one of the founders of the *Verein für Sozialpolitik,* and has since been known as a leading "socialist of the chair." His connection with the *Verein für Sozialpolitik* lasted but a few years. His opinions respecting the function of the state as an agent in effecting social reforms were too radical even for his associates, and he finally withdrew, leaving the field to Schmoller, Brentano and their followers. . . .

The energy and earnestness that pervades all of Professor Wagner's actions is, the reader may be sure, rather intensified than otherwise when he mounts the rostrum. His appearance, when seated behind his high desk delivering a lecture, is striking enough. His features are prominent, and furnish a good index of his character. In his chin and mouth, only partially concealed by his thick and slightly grizzled mustache, one reads the man of prompt action and of resolute will, a born soldier in a nation of soldiers. The facial resemblance between Wagner and Bismarck, not so striking at present as formerly I believe, has often been remarked upon. When lecturing, his delivery is rapid and emphatic, his voice harsh but not unpleasant. He uses his notes only for occasional reference, being enabled by his remarkable memory to carry the substance of a two-hour lecture in his head without apparent effort. As a lecturer, he, like many of his colleagues, is open to the criticism of paying too much attention to the matter and too little to the form of his utterances. To his unusually logical mind all facts come in groups, classified in advance. His lectures are so filled with *erstens* [first] and *zweitens* [second] that the hearer is apt to lose the kernel of his thought altogether in trying to keep clearly in his head its proper position in the hierarchy of ideas presented. As regards the matter of his lectures, it is needless to say much to anyone acquainted with his writings; a wealth of striking illustrations and interesting facts borrowed from the economic histories of all countries, great succinctness of statement and logicalness of treatment—are characteristic features.

The fundamental idea that pervades and gives unity to Wagner's economic system is the "social" idea. Analyzing the history of the development of economic thought, he sees, on the one hand, the system of *individualism,* dating back to the Physiocrats and Adam Smith, the fundamental tenet of which is the *"laissez-faire"* doctrine; on the other, the doctrines of the socialists and communists, representing a timely reaction from the individualism of the Classical school, but, as is usual with reactions, going too far to the other extreme. The standpoint of socialism he accepts as the only rational standpoint, i.e., the good of the community, of society, must be the starting point in political economy, and not the good of the individual or of any group of individuals. But, starting out with this principle, it is necessary to take strict account of existing institutions on the one hand, and of the nature of man on the other. In neglecting this latter point, i.e., in failing to ground economics upon a rational system of psychology, socialism has committed its cardinal error. Wagner prides himself upon appreciating and adopting in his own system what is best in both extreme positions. He judges everything from the social standpoint; he regards, for example, the juster distribution of incomes as a legitimate motive for guiding the action of a state in laying its taxes, but he by no means overlooks the importance of self-interest as one of the principal impelling motives to all human action.

The practical conclusions which he draws from such a line of reasoning may be briefly summarized as follows:

The institutions of private law, and especially private property, are justifiable only so long as they serve the best interests of society; there is nothing inviolable or sacred about them; in fact, as at present existing, they are very far from fulfilling the requirements of an ideal society. Social and economic reform must be preceded by the reform of the legal ideas which constitute the very framework of society. By reform, however, he does not understand any such radical measure as, for example, the abolition of the institution of private property, but rather such modifications in this and other existing legal institutions as shall cause them to better serve the interests of society, without at the same time neglecting self-interest as the chief economic motive of all action.

In such a reform the state is assigned by Wagner to a very important role. The "good-of-the-whole" is the only justifiable principle by which to guide state actions.[7] It is in this sense and this sense only that Professor Wagner is a "state socialist" or a "socialist-of-the-chair," as are many other leading German professors, such as Professor Schäffle. They form no school—even the name was thrust upon them by hostile critics—but nonetheless they represent a dominant factor in German economic thought. . . .

On the subject of method, Professor Wagner's views coincide almost exactly with those of Professor Marshall already quoted.[8] He expressly says,[9] however, that he has much more sympathy for the earnest attitude assumed by Professor Carl Menger towards the methodological question than for the critically indifferent attitude of his colleague, Professor Schmoller. . . .

Professor Wagner's conception of a *Seminar* is that of a course in which the professor takes for the time the minor role of director and the students themselves become the lecturers. Upon the occasion of our second meeting, the director submitted to each one of us in turn a series of questions in regard to our former work in economics, our preferences in the science, and the motives which had led us to enter his course.

Each of us having given a short sketch of his mental history, and declared his preferences in the economic field, the director next took up the subject of *Arbeiten* [work, assignments]. The difficult task of assigning work to such as desired it was performed by Professor Wagner in a way to excite general admiration. . . . Each one was, before the evening was over, assigned his special task and each one was, apparently, satisfied. By the time the first paper was read, dates had been fixed for the reading of all the rest. Thus at the very outset, a program for the whole semester was arranged from which only slight variations were subsequently made. . . .

Professor Wagner's success as a teacher is due very largely to the sincerity and earnestness of his character. In spite of a manner at times rather brusque and a little repelling, he always inspires his students with confidence and respect. The "social" idea which is the central thought in his economic system is also the guiding principle of his life. In him the pupil recognizes not merely a great scholar but a noble character. His example is fitted to inspire right-living quite as much as is his teaching to inculcate right-thinking.

In Professor Schmoller we have quite another type of *Gelehrter*

[7] For a more complete statement of Wagner's views, see his *Grundlagender Volkswirtschaft*. Leipzig, 1892, especially pp. 5–67.

[8] Compare his *Grundlagen*, p. 18.

[9] *Idem.*, *Einleitung*, p. vii, and Vol. 1, No. 1 of the *Journal of Political Economy*, p. 110.

[scholar]. Though Professor Wagner's junior by three years, he appears the older of the two. Shorter in stature but no less erect and martial in his carriage, with a flowing white beard and white hair, Professor Schmoller presents a personality to be remembered. Of a type more common to Gaul than to Germania, he seems to find in his sense of humor, in his artistic appreciation of fine sayings and fine writings, compensation for his lack of great convictions. In his graceful literary style we find his great point of superiority over so many of his German colleagues. His lectures are attractive, not so much for the truths they contain, however weighty these may be, as because of the manner in which these truths are expressed.

In his course upon "general" economics, it would seem almost a sarcasm to speak of it as upon "theoretical" economics. He devotes the first few lectures to explaining the nature of political economy and its relation to kindred sciences and to defining the terms which the economist employs. Following this introductory portion comes the most valuable and characteristic part of his whole course, a series of lectures upon the rise and development of human institutions. He points out that the three "norms" of any society are its morals, its customs, and its laws; these constitute the framework within which each of the social sciences must be built up.

His characterization of modern industrial society is masterly. He treats at length and strictly in accordance with the historical method the subjects of population and division of labor. Here the master historian and statistician shows himself. The manner in which he picks out of the great mass of existing material only those facts and figures essential to his purpose and in which he groups this selected matter so as to draw from it the most far-reaching conclusions and to give to the student not merely a valuable set of historical notes, but also a grasp of the deeply underlying principles and tendencies, is truly admirable. Throughout, Schmoller shows himself not merely an historian, but also a philosopher. He has a fondness for philosophical terms and for indulging in excursions outside of his proper field. Herbert Spencer is the English author whom he most frequently quotes. He is inclined, "almost" he says, to ascribe to Adam Smith's *Theory of the Moral Sentiments* greater value than to his *Wealth of Nations.* Here and everywhere we see the two sides to his economic thinking; on the one hand the historian and statistician, upon the other the idealist, who joins the what-is with the what-ought-to-be and forms out of the two a most rosy picture of the future of the human race. In the first case we see the economist, in the second the man.

Up to this point his lectures upon "general" economics had been models of their kind. When, however, he took up what to another would have been theoretical political economy and attempted to treat it also simply descriptively, the listener was at once conscious of the change. At this point came the crucial test for Schmoller's theory of method, and at this point, it seemed to me, his theory broke down conspicuously.

In his treatment of value and price he showed his acquaintance with the work of the Austrians by freely borrowing their results, not however as consequences of a long and difficult chain of deductive reasoning, but simply as the obvious inferences from his own description of market phenomena. In this part of his lectures, the student meets only confusion, loose definitions, description instead of careful analysis, and conclusions arrived at, no one knows exactly how. His elucidation of the action of demand and supply in fixing price seemed to me especially unhappy.

When he proceeds to the history and technique of money, the hearer almost sighs with relief. He completed his course with a sketch of the laboring class and a descriptive account of wages and of the labor movement.

In his course upon "the nature and history of economic 'undertaking' and the forms of 'undertaking,'" Professor Schmoller has a subject after his own heart. Here his particular method of treatment is exactly at home and the fruitfulness of its application in the hands of such a master need not be dwelt upon.

However opposed one may be to some of the ideas of Professor Schmoller, one cannot but be impressed by the consummate manner in which he presents them. His importance and influence in German economics cannot be appreciated by one who has never heard him lecture. As editor of a leading economic journal, in the columns of which he himself often figures, sometimes as an original investigator, more often as a graceful and acute critic, he enjoys a conspicuously advantageous position for keeping his ideas constantly before the reading public, and for this reason, perhaps, he has been able to make a showing of strength upon his side in the *Methodenstreit* which his position hardly warrants.
. . .

University of Vienna:

The change from the straightness of Berlin streets and the regularity of Berlin architecture to the pleasing variety afforded by Viennese *Ringstrassen* and Viennese palaces is no less striking to the tourists, than is the change from the University of Berlin to the University of Vienna to the political economist. In Berlin political economy figures as one of the liberal sciences belonging to the philosophical faculty, as a science having closer affiliations with philosophy than with law. Here in Vienna political economy is a study belonging to the law department. A certain amount of work in it is required of all jurists and, in consequence, the benches in the economic lecture-rooms are crowded with law students. Professor Wagner used to complain in Berlin because so few jurists were attracted into the economic work there; here in Vienna the very opposite complaint might be raised. All the students of economics seem to be jurists. . . .

In all, nine courses are offered at the University of Vienna, occupying just nineteen hours a week, compared with the nineteen courses occupying forty-eight hours a week offered at Berlin, certainly a rather meager showing.[10] How is this difference to be explained? In part, quite simply. Berlin enrolls annually nearly one-third more students[11] and accordingly should be able to offer a more varied and complete course of study than does Vienna. Secondly, the work in economics at Vienna is temporarily crippled, owing to the fact that the chair occupied formerly by Brentano and more recently by Miaskowski, has for two years remained vacant.[12] It may be questioned, however, if these two causes sufficiently explain the comparative neglect of economic science that is apparent here. A third and really more vital reason is found in the fact that here in Vienna, and especially is this true of the law faculty, very much of the work preliminary to a degree is expressly prescribed. The student is given very little time for courses not directly necessary as a part of his preparation for the examinations. In consequence the required courses are disproportionately crowded; those not required have a severe struggle for existence. The demand for a varied economic diet does not exist here as it does in Berlin, and in consequence the supply is also lacking.[13] Coming to details, it will be noticed that all of the courses given here this semester with the exception of three, i.e., the general course of Professor Menger, the seminar of Professor Böhm-

---

[10] Comparing a winter semester with a summer semester is, to be sure, not exactly fair to Berlin.

[11] According to official figures there were at Berlin during the calendar year 1890–91 an average for each semester of 7,613 students; at Vienna for the same period only 5,670 students.

[12] Professor von Philippovich, a born Viennese, has quite recently accepted a call from his post at Freiburg to fill this vacant chair. He is himself a follower of Menger on questions of method and of general theory, so that beginning with next year we will no doubt see a harmonious course offered here in economics.

[13] The percentage of *Privatdozenten* [private lecturers] is greater at Vienna than at Berlin, and therefore we would not expect quite the same number of hours of instruction.

Bawerk, and the one-hour course on credit and banking of Dr. Zuck-erkandl, deal either with statistics or with some aspect of socialism. This fact is further evidence of the absence of a demand on the part of the student body for a really comprehensive course in economics.

It has been Professor Menger's custom to deliver a course of five lectures a week upon general economics in the winter semester, and to continue this with a course of the same length upon public finance during the summer semester. In addition he held last year a seminar for two hours a week for general economics and finance. This semester, Professor Böhm-Bawerk conducts the seminar and, in consequence, Professor Menger's pedagogic activity is limited to his general lecture course.

Professor Menger carries his fifty-three years lightly enough. In lecturing he rarely uses his notes except to verify a quotation or a date. His ideas seem to come to him as he speaks and are expressed in language so clear and simple, and emphasized with gestures so appropriate, that it is a pleasure to follow him. The student feels that he is being led instead of driven, and when a conclusion is reached it comes into his mind not as something from without, but as the obvious consequence of his own mental processes. It is said that those who attend Professor Menger's lectures regularly need no other preparation for their final examination in political economy, and I can readily believe it. I have seldom, if ever, heard a lecturer who possessed the same talent for combining clearness and simplicity of statement with philosophical breadth of view. His lectures are seldom "over the heads" of his dullest students, and yet always contain instruction for the brightest.

The majority of Professor Menger's hearers are taking his course as a part of their required work. It is his task, therefore, to give them in the eighty-odd lectures which he delivers, a general view of economics, an idea not merely of economic principles, but also of the history of economic thought and of economic practice. He introduces his course with a vivid sketch of the characteristic features of modern industrial society, emphasizing especially its dependence upon existing legal institutions. Political economy is then defined and its relation to kindred sciences specified. Following, he takes up the history of the development of economic ideas. Commencing with the ideas of Plato and Aristotle, he explains most happily the economic doctrines of various thinkers and schools down to most modern times. In this part of his course he has occasion to give evidence of his profound knowledge of economic literature. In his notes concerning rare editions and unfamiliar bits of bibliography one sees the book-lover and the antiquarian.

He has the happy faculty of giving life to the ideas and the authors he is discussing. The economic doctrines of the old Mercantilists and the Physiocrats are not, as explained by him, the impossible combinations of fallacies and absurdities one still finds in many textbooks, but the simple products of the times which gave them birth, correct to a large extent in their practical conclusions, if deceived in their premises. And he is not satisfied with simply explaining and criticizing exploded theories, but impresses them vividly upon the minds of his hearers by pointing out, here and there, survivals of these old theories in the popular economics of today.

Coming down to contemporary economists and economic thought, he displays a freedom in treatment and objectivity in criticism uncommon in Germany. The isolated position occupied by Professor Menger here at Vienna enables him to speak with more candor and openness of his German contemporaries in his lectures than they venture to use in speaking of each other. Especially interesting to the foreign student is his characterization of the Historical school and of *Kathedersozialismus,* the forerunners of which last he finds in Simonde de Sismondi and J. S. Mill. He closes his historical sketch with six lectures upon socialism and communism and the role they have played in economic literature.

Such an extended historical sketch as he gives would invite criticism of his method of treatment as being too minute for a general course on political economy were it not for the masterly manner in which Professor Menger unites in these lectures the present with the past. He knows his students thoroughly and has, no doubt, learned from experience that ideas are readily comprehended when unfolded to the individual mind, not dogmatically, but in the same order in which history shows them to have been unfolded to the race. His success in developing his own ideas and theories, side by side with those which he is nominally discussing, is certainly remarkable and answers all criticism in advance.

The latter half of his course is devoted to the expounding of his own theoretical system. The starting point in political economy is to him the relation between human wants and the goods, be they material or immaterial, upon which depends the satisfaction of these wants. The fact that there are more wants than means of satisfying them gives rise to the phenomenon of value. Thus the value of any particular good to any particular individual is simply his estimation of the importance of the want the satisfaction of which depends upon *that* good. It is therefore a resultant of the utility and scarcity of the good in question. The classification of wants on the basis of their intensities next takes up his attention as a preliminary step leading to the law of "marginal utility." With the help of this law he explains the Austrian theory of value and price. These theories he applies in turn to the problems met with in exchange and distribution much as in his *Grundsätze der Volkswirtschafts-lehre*.[14]

One can scarcely say too much in praise of Professor Menger as a teacher. His great popularity with his students and the success that has attended his efforts to gather around himself talented young men, who sympathize with his fundamental views, are sufficient evidence of his genius in this direction. Among the several thousand volumes upon Professor Menger's shelves will be found almost every work upon economics that is likely to interest the student of general theory, not only in German, but also in English, French, Italian, and even Dutch. The library is specially rich in works upon method, upon money, upon public finance, and in complete files of economic journals. To have access to such a collection of books is itself a boon of inestimable value. Add to it the advice and guidance of such a man as Professor Menger, and the reader will understand some of the attractions which induce not a few economic students to come here to Vienna in preference even to going to Berlin.

In Professor Böhm-Bawerk's seminar we have a source of even greater interest to the specialist than the general course of Professor Menger which we have just described. Professor Böhm-Bawerk, although only forty-two years of age, is already known to economists of all countries as one of the most prominent economists of the Austrian school. To Professor Menger belongs the supreme credit of having originated in their broad outlines all of the ideas that characterize this school. Professor Böhm-Bawerk, however, has helped more than anyone else to popularize these ideas and follow them out to their logical but more remote consequences. Shortly after receiving an appointment to an important post in the finance department, Professor Böhm-Bawerk was given the title of honorary professor in the University of Vienna. It is in this latter capacity that he conducts the economic seminar.

The meetings of the economic seminar occur this semester every Friday at five o'clock and last usually an hour and a half. They are held in a simple lecture room accommodating some fifty or sixty students and usually fairly well filled. Adjoining is a small room containing the seminar library of a few hundred standard works. Alas, periodicals are altogether lacking. The thirty-five or forty students who assembled at the first meeting appeared to be nearly all Austrians. All ages and conditions seem to be represented, from the care-free corps student to the

---

[14] English translation, *Principles of Economics* (Free Press of Glencoe, 1950; Libertarian Press, 1994).

hard-working graduate looking forward to higher academic honors. At the opening exercise Professor Böhm-Bawerk lost no time in explaining the purpose of the course. The wages question was to be our subject: its exhaustive, historical and critical discussion and, as far as possible, its solution, our object. Papers should be presented upon the various wages theories that have gained prominence from the time when the question first received scientific attention; upon the basis of these, discussion was to be engaged in until positive conclusions should be reached. Original theories were to be given a hearing as soon as the material to be found in literature had been disposed of.

The reader will observe at once that his is quite another sort of seminar from that we have seen Professor Wagner conducting in Berlin. To the latter a seminar is a course in which all sorts of original investigations in any particular field are to be given a hearing; to Professor Böhm-Bawerk it has a more special character—some particular topic is to be taken and studied by a number of students collectively; every student present is supposed to be especially interested in the topic under consideration and to take an active part in the debate; no point is to be abandoned until all are agreed that it has been sufficiently discussed. The presentation of papers is simply secondary; they are designed to introduce, but never to take the place of, the general debate which is to follow. The purpose of such a seminar as Professor Böhm-Bawerk offers makes its attainment much more certain than in a general seminar like Professor Wagner's. When all are studying the same subject, all must be intelligently interested in such papers as are presented, and all must learn something from the different points of view brought out in the debate.

Already, at our second meeting, the first paper was presented, giving a rapid historical sketch of wages theories and stating the problem which such theories have to solve. The debate which followed was to me an agreeable surprise. The five or six students who took part in it displayed a talent for succinct and forcible statement and for critical analysis for which my previous experience with German seminars had little prepared me. In the summary with which the director closed the discussion, the subjects upon which special papers should be presented were enumerated.

Up to the present time papers have been presented upon the "minimum-of-existence-theory" of wages, the "cost-of-production-theory" of wages, and the "wages-fund theory." The discussions have been, for the most part, interesting and valuable though, as usual in a seminar, repetitions are frequent, and much superfluous matter is introduced. Nearly all of the members of the seminar are old pupils, either of Professor Menger or of Professor Böhm-Bawerk, and all are eager partisans of the Austrian school. It is this that gives a certain unity to the various ideas and points of view that find expression in the debates, and that constitutes the most attractive and interesting feature of the course to the stranger.

Here in Vienna the marginal utility theory of value is anything but an "academic plaything."[15] It is through the application of this theory to the general problem of distribution that a solution of the wages question is expected, insofar as it is possible to find any purely economic theory to account for a phenomenon in the production of which so many uneconomic elements are prominent factors. Whether, as a final result of this careful discussion of the wages question in all its bearings, a positive conclusion, to which all are ready to subscribe, will be arrived at or not, is a matter of comparatively slight importance. The value of the course consists in the encouragement it gives to original thinking and in the sharpening effect it has upon the critical faculties of all those who take part in it. It has been to me the most valuable economics course I have had in Germany. I cannot well say more. . . .

In almost every respect the material facilities for economic work afforded the specialist at Berlin, especially the well-equipped libraries offering students some 400,000 books and periodicals in many languages, are decidedly superior to those afforded him here at Vienna, which are only moderately good. In Vienna, however, Professor Menger allows students to use his personal 5,000 volume library. To conclude from this fact, however, that more is to be gained by a semester at the former place than by a semester here, would be unwarranted. It all depends upon what the student wants. If he is interested especially in economic history, in social questions, or in practical economics and public finance, Berlin undoubtedly will give the greater satisfaction. If, on the other hand, he is interested in general theory, the fundamental questions of the science such as the methodological question, or the history of economic dogma and the development of economic theory, the balance is as unquestionably in favor of Vienna.

He will find here a remarkably able corps of teachers, all professing substantially the same beliefs and economic doctrines, and all striving to apply these doctrines to the reform of economic science. What has already been done in the direction of recasting general economic theory on the basis of the marginal utility theory of value is only a foretaste of what yet remains to be done.

---

[15] It is thus that Ingram characterizes the similar ideas advanced by Jevons in England. Cf. History of Political Economy, London, 1888, p. 234.

Carl Menger and the Austrian School of Economics[1]

by Ludwig von Mises

On the day when the memorial to Carl Menger is to be unveiled in the courtyard of the University of Vienna, it seems appropriate to take a look at the work accomplished by Menger, founder of the "Austrian School of Economics." This is by no means merely a posthumous tribute to persons who are dead and gone. Even though those who developed the Austrian school are no longer with us, their work survives as firm as a rock and it still continues. What they contributed has become the basis of all scientific effort in economic theory. Every economic thought today is connected with what Menger and his school demonstrated. 1871, the date of the publication of Menger's first scientific work, *Principles of Economics*, is usually considered the opening of a new epoch in the history of our science.

No place would be better than the columns of the *Neue Freie Presse* to review briefly for a larger audience the work of the Austrian school. Carl Menger himself, as well as all the others closely or more loosely associated with the older Austrian school—Eugen von Böhm-Bawerk, Friedrich von Wieser, Robert Zuckerkandl, Emil Sax, Robert Meyer, Johann Komorzynski, Rudolf Auspitz, Richard Lieben—often availed themselves of the pages of the *Neue Freie Presse* to discuss economic and political events of the day and to report on the results of their theoretical analyses.

I

The knowledge that prices, wages, and interest rates are clearly determined through the marketplace, even within very narrow margins, and that the market price functions as a regulator of production, was developed in the 18th century by the Physiocrats in France and by the Scots David Hume and Adam Smith. This knowledge became the historical foundation of scientific economics. Where previously men had seen only chance and caprice in economic affairs, they came to recognize regularity. The Classical school of economics, which reached its

---

[1] *Neue Freie Presse* (Vienna), January 29/30, 1929. Translated from the German.

peak in the works of David Ricardo, considered its task to be to elaborate a comprehensive system of catallactics, a theory of exchange and income.

The recognition brought to light by theoretical investigation led to important conclusions for economic policy. People began to realize that the interventions, by which governments sought to direct the economic forces in a certain way to attain some particular goal, must fail. By no means can the fixing of maximum prices assure the provisioning of the people at the cheapest possible prices; if the official order is actually obeyed, it leads to a contraction, if not to a complete halt, of the shipment to the market of the commodities concerned; thus the intervention accomplishes the very opposite of what had been intended. The situation is similar with respect to the political regulation of wages and interest rates, as well as with regard to interventions in international trade. Mercantilism believed that to assure equilibrium in foreign trade measures of trade policy (tariffs, embargoes, etc.) were necessary. Ricardo proved that equilibrium always reestablishes itself automatically, that measures of trade policy to protect a monetary standard not destroyed by inflation are superfluous, and that they are incapable also of halting an inflation-caused downward slide of purchasing power. Political measures aimed at trade policy divert production away from opportunities that take advantage of the most advantageous natural conditions of production, reducing the economic productivity of labor as a result and thus depressing the living standards of the masses.

In the eyes of Classical economics interventionism seemed nonsensical in every respect. The continual improvement in the well-being of all classes may be expected, not from government interventions which only hinder and hamper economic development, but from the free flow of all forces. So the political program of liberalism, which advocated free trade in domestic as well as international economic policy, is built on the foundation of Classical economic theory.

Whoever wants to struggle against liberalism, must attempt to refute these conclusions. But that is impossible. The aspect of Classical economic theory on which liberalism rests cannot be shaken. Only one way remains for the opponents of liberalism: they must reject on principle, as the German Historical school of political science does, any knowledge of the social economy which claims general validity for its tenets; only economic history and economic description are considered of value; fundamental investigations of the interconnectedness of economic phenomena are declared to be "abstract" and "unscientific."

After Walter Bagehot, whose reputation as a political economist rests on his renowned book on the London money market, *Lombard*

Street, had already struggled against these errors in the mid-1870s, Menger came forward in 1883 with his *Untersuchungen über die Methode der Socialwissenschaften* [Investigations into the Methods of the Social Sciences]. The debates associated with this book, which have come to be known as the *Methodenstreit*, exposed the objections raised by historicism against the logical and methodological correctness of the existence of generally valid knowledge in the field of economics. Theoretical ideas and principles, the general validity of which is maintained even if not so recognized, are found in every economic historical investigation or description. Without a consideration of theory, it is impossible to assert anything about anything. In every statement about commodity prices, taxes, socio-political measures or group interests, "theory" must necessarily be included. If the school of academic socialists has failed to notice this, that does not mean they have operated without theory. It only means they have relinquished any claim to investigate the correctness of their theories in advance, to think them through to their logical conclusions, to integrate them into a system, to explore their irrefutability and their logical consistency, and to check them against the facts. Instead of useful, irrefutable theories, therefore, the school has based its investigations on untenable, long-since repudiated errors which are full of contradictions. And these it has presented as the outcome of its efforts.

To pursue economic theory means simply to examine all assertions concerning economics, again and again, to examine them very critically on their merit, using every intellectual means available.

II

Classical economics was unable to solve the problem of price formation satisfactorily. To accomplish this, it is obvious that the basis of the evaluations, which determine the configuration of the prices of goods, derive from their utility (their usefulness for the satisfaction of human needs). However, that presented a difficulty which the Classicists, in spite of their ingenuity, were unable to overcome. Many of the most useful goods, such as iron, coal, or bread, have little value on the market; goods such as water or air are not even considered to have any value at all. On the other hand, some less useful commodities, precious stones for instance, are highly valued. In view of the failure of all their efforts to explain this antinomy, the Classicists seized on other explanations of value, but without artificial help none of these could be thought through to an irrefutable conclusion. Apparently nothing seemed to work.

Then Menger appeared on the scene with his ingenious first book which overcame the supposed antinomy of value. It is not the significance of the entire class of goods, which determines value, but the significance of precisely that portion of a good that is at one's disposal. Since we ascribe to every individual portion of a given supply only the importance of the want-satisfaction it has brought about, then with respect to every individual class of needs the urgency of further gratification diminishes with progressive satisfaction; thus we value each concrete aliquot [fractional] portion according to the importance of the last, i.e., the least important, concrete need which can be satisfied by the still available supply, that is to its marginal utility. In this way, the formation of the prices of goods of the first order, i.e., goods for immediate use and for consumption, may be traced to the subjective values of consumers. The formation of the prices of goods of the higher orders (also known as factors of production or operational goods) including wages, prices for labor power, i.e., goods needed for the production of consumers' goods and luxury goods, are also traced back to the prices of the goods of the first order. Thus in the final analysis it is the consumers who determine and who pay the prices of the means of production and wages. To accomplish this calculation is the task of accounting theory which deals specifically with prices, wages, interest, and entrepreneurial profit.

Using the knowledge already won by the Classicals, Menger and his successors erected on the new foundation a comprehensive system interpreting all economic phenomena.

III

Almost at the same time as Menger, and independently of him, the Englishman William Stanley Jevons and the Frenchman Léon Walras working in Lausanne [Switzerland] expounded similar theories. After some time had passed, time which every new idea needs to be accepted, the subjectivist marginal utility theory became victorious worldwide. Menger was luckier than his important forerunner, the Prussian government official Hermann Heinrich Gossen; Menger's theory gained the recognition of economists throughout the entire world. The ideas of the Austrian school were developed in the United States especially by John Bates Clark, founder of the renowned American school. Clark, like Heinrich Oswalt in Frankfurt and Richard Reisch, is a worthy associate of the Economic Society of Vienna. The theory soon flourished also in the Netherlands and the Scandinavian countries. And successful scientific work based on it appeared in Italy.

Menger did not found a school in the usual sense of the word. He stood too high and thought too much of the worth of science to use the paltry means by which others seek to promote themselves. He inquired, wrote and taught. And the best who have worked in the Austrian state and economy in recent decades have been products of that school. Optimistic like all liberals, Menger fully expected that reason must finally prevail. Before long Menger had two companions who stood with him, two men who followed in his footsteps, both a decade younger than Menger—Eugen von Böhm-Bawerk and Friedrich von Wieser. Both were the same age, had been friends from youth, were bound together as brothers-in-law, and were related also by conviction, character, and culture. As scientific personalities, however, they were both as different as two equally aspiring contemporaries could be. Yet each in his own way began working where Menger left off. Working as mature men with Menger's works at hand, they succeeded in solving problems. Their names are now inseparably linked to Menger's in the history of our science.

Now these two men have also completed their work and their lives. A new generation is coming along. A collection of exceptional scientific investigations has been published in recent years by men who have not yet reached their thirties, showing that Austria is unwilling to relinquish her priority as a source of important economic contributions.

IV

The Historical school of academic socialism and of "economic political science" has not allowed itself to be interrupted by the critical and positive work of the Austrian school any more than it has by the foreign interventionist school. The members of the German Historical school, confident in the political power guaranteed them by government and political parties, continue to look down contemptuously on serious theoretical work; and they continue calmly to publish their work on the omnipotence of the state over the economy.

The economic-political experiments put into effect during the War [World War I] and the early post-war years carried interventionism and statism to a peak. Everything that was tried—maximum prices, the command economy, inflation—turned out just as foreseen by the theoreticians, the theoreticians who are despised by government officials and adherents of the Historical school. Yet the opponents of "abstract, inappropriate, Austrian value theory" still tried stubbornly to maintain their point of view. How far they went in their delusion is illustrated by the fact that one of them renowned as a monetary authority, Bank

Director Bendixen, announced that he believed that the undervaluation abroad of the German currency during the War was "to a certain extent even desirable because it made it possible for us to purchase foreign goods at an advantageous rate."

Finally, however, a reaction must set in. The Historical school's anti-theoretical position is beginning to be rejected. The decade-long neglect of theoretical studies had led to the remarkable result that the German public must look to a foreigner, the Swede Gustav Cassel, for a principled explanation of the problems of economic life. For example, Cassel related to German newspaper readers, not only the old purchasing power parity theory of exchange rates first developed by Ricardo, but also the suggestion that lasting unemployment is a necessary consequence of union wage policy. Cassel expounded in his theoretical works the theory of the subjectivist school, even if he expressed it a little differently and at times somewhat awkwardly so that it is not exactly worth accepting in every detail.

Though the camp followers of the Historical school still try to set forth their old theme of the end or collapse of marginal theory, one cannot fail but recognize, however, that to an increasing extent the ideas and thoughts of the Austrian school are penetrating the treatises of today's younger political economists, even in the German Reich. The work of Menger and his friends has become the foundation of the entire modern science of economics.

The Historical Setting of the Austrian School of Economics*

by Ludwig von Mises

I. Carl Menger and the Austrian School of Economics

1. The Beginnings

What is known as the "Austrian School of Economics" started in 1871 when Carl Menger published a slender volume under the title *Grundsätze der Volkswirthschaftslehre.*

It is customary to trace the influence that the milieu exerted upon the achievements of genius. People like to ascribe the exploits of a man of genius, at least to some extent, to the operation of his environment and to the climate of opinion of his age and his country. Whatever this method may accomplish in some cases, there is no doubt that it is inapplicable with regard to those Austrians whose thoughts, ideas and doctrines matter for mankind. Bernard Bolzano, Gregor Mendel, and Sigmund Freud were not stimulated by their relatives, teachers, colleagues or friends. Their exertions did not meet with sympathy on the part of their contemporary countrymen and the government of their country. Bolzano and Mendel carried on their main work in surroundings which, as far as their special fields are concerned, could be called an intellectual desert, and they died long before people began to divine the worth of their contributions. Freud was laughed at when he first made public his doctrines in the Vienna Medical Association.

One may say that the theory of subjectivism and marginalism that Carl Menger developed was in the air. It had been foreshadowed by several forerunners. Besides, about the same time Menger wrote and published his book, William Stanley Jevons and Léon Walras also wrote and published books which expounded the concept of marginal utility. However this may be, it is certain that none of his teachers, friends, or colleagues took any interest in the problems that excited Menger. Some time before the outbreak of the first World War when I told him about the informal but regular meetings in which we younger Vienna econo-

---

* Originally published by Arlington House (1969). Reprinted with permission.

mists used to discuss problems of economic theory, he pensively observed: "When I was your age, nobody in Vienna cared about these things." Until the end of the 1870s there was no "Austrian School." There was only Carl Menger.

Eugen von Böhm-Bawerk and Friedrich von Wieser never studied with Menger. They had finished their studies at the University of Vienna before Menger began to lecture as a *Privatdozent*. What they learned from Menger, they got from studying the *Grundsätze*. When they returned to Austria after some time spent at German universities, especially in the seminar of Karl Knies in Heidelberg, and published their first books, they were appointed to teach economics at the Universities of Innsbruck and Prague respectively. Very soon some younger men who had gone through Menger's seminar and had been exposed to his personal influence, enlarged the number of authors who contributed to economic inquiry. People abroad began to refer to these authors as "the Austrians." But the designation "Austrian School of Economics" was used only later, when their antagonism to the German Historical school came into the open after the publication, in 1883, of Menger's second book, *Untersuchungen über die Methode der Socialwissenschaften und der Politischen Oekonomie insbesondere.*

2. The Austrian School of Economics and the Austrian Universities

The Austrian Cabinet in whose journalistic department Menger served in the early 1870s—before his appointment in 1873 as assistant professor at the University of Vienna—was composed of members of the Liberal Party that stood for civil liberties, representative government, equality of all citizens under the law, sound money, and free trade. At the end of the 1870s the Liberal Party was evicted by an alliance of the Church, the princes and counts of the Czech and Polish aristocracy, and the nationalist parties of the various Slavonic nationalities. This coalition was opposed to all the ideals which the Liberals had supported. However, until the disintegration of the Habsburg Empire in 1918, the Constitution which the Liberals had induced the Emperor to accept in 1867 and the fundamental laws that complemented it remained by and large valid.

In the climate of freedom that these statutes warranted, Vienna became a center of the harbingers of new ways of thinking. From the middle of the sixteenth to the end of the eighteenth century Austria was foreign to the intellectual effort of Europe. Nobody in Vienna—and still less in other parts of the Austrian dominions—cared for the philosophy, literature, and science of Western Europe. When Leibniz and later

David Hume visited Vienna, no indigenes were to be found there who would have been interested in their work.[1] With the exception of Bolzano, no Austrian before the second part of the nineteenth century contributed anything of importance to the philosophical or the historical sciences.

But when the Liberals had removed the fetters that had prevented any intellectual effort, when they had abolished censorship and had denounced the concordat, eminent minds began to converge toward Vienna. Some came from Germany—like the philosophers Lorenz von Stein and Rudolf von Jhering—but most of them came from the Austrian provinces; a few were born Viennese. There was no conformity among these leaders, nor among their followers. Brentano, the ex-Dominican, inaugurated a line of thought that finally led to Husserl's phenomenology. Mach was the exponent of a philosophy that resulted in the logical positivism of Schlick, Carnap, and their "Vienna Circle." Breuer, Freud, and Adler interpreted neurotic phenomena in a way radically different from the methods of Krafft-Ebing and Wagner-Jauregg.

The Austrian "Ministry of Worship and Instruction" looked askance upon all these endeavors. Since the early 1880s the Cabinet Minister and the personnel of this department had been chosen from the most reliable conservatives and foes of all modern ideas and political institutions. They had nothing but contempt for what in their eyes were "outlandish fads." They would have liked to bar the universities from access to all this innovation.

But the power of the administration was seriously restricted by three "privileges" which the universities had acquired under the impact of the Liberal ideas. The professors were civil servants and, like all other civil servants, bound to obey the orders issued by their superiors, i.e., the Cabinet Minister and his aides. However, these superiors did not have the right to interfere with the content of the doctrines taught in the classes and seminars. In this regard the professors enjoyed the much talked about "academic freedom." Furthermore, the Minister was obliged—although this obligation had never been unambiguously stated—to comply in appointing professors, or to speak more precisely in suggesting to the Emperor the appointment of a professor, with the suggestions made by the faculty concerned. Finally there was the institution of the *Privatdozent*. A doctor who had published a scholarly book could ask the faculty to admit him as a free and private teacher of his discipline. If the faculty decided in favor of the petitioner, the consent

---

[1] The only contemporary Viennese who appreciated the philosophic work of Leibniz was Prince Eugene of Savoy, scion of a French family, born and educated in France.

of the Minister was still required. In practice this consent was, before the days of the Schuschnigg regime, always given. The duly admitted *Privatdozent* was not, in this capacity, a civil servant. Even if the title of professor was accorded to him, he did not receive any compensation from the government. A few *Privatdozents* could live from their own funds. Most of them worked for their living. Their right to collect the fees paid by the students who attended their courses was in most cases practically valueless.

The effect of this arrangement of academic affairs was that the councils of the professors enjoyed almost unlimited autonomy in the management of their schools. Economics was taught at the Schools of Law and Social Sciences (*Rechts und staatswissenschaftliche Fakultäten*) of the universities. At most of these universities there were two chairs of economics. If one of these chairs became vacant, a body of lawyers had—with the cooperation at most of one economist—to choose the future incumbent. Thus the decision rested with non-economists. It may be fairly assumed that these professors of law were guided by the best intentions. But they were not economists. They had to choose between two opposed schools of thought, the Austrian school on the one hand, and the allegedly "modern" Historical school as taught at the universities of the German Reich on the other hand. Even if no political and nationalistic prepossessions had disturbed their judgment, they could not help becoming somewhat suspicious of a line of thought which the professors of the universities of the German Reich dubbed specifically Austrian. Never before had any new mode of thinking originated in Austria. The Austrian universities had been sterile until—after the revolution of 1848—they had been reorganized according to the model of the German universities. For people who were not familiar with economics, the predicate "Austrian" as applied to a doctrine carried strong overtones of the dark days of the counter-reformation and of Metternich. To an Austrian intellectual, nothing could appear more disastrous than a relapse of his country into the spiritual inanity of the good old days.

Carl Menger, Wieser, and Böhm-Bawerk had obtained their chairs in Vienna, Prague, and Innsbruck before the *Methodenstreit* had begun to appear in the opinion of the Austrian laymen as a conflict between "modern" science and Austrian "backwardness." Their colleagues had no personal grudge against them. But whenever possible they tried to bring followers of the Historical school from Germany to the Austrian universities. Those whom the world called the "Austrian economists" were, in the Austrian universities, somewhat reluctantly tolerated outsiders.

3. The Austrian School in the Intellectual Life of Austria

The more distinguished among the French and German universities were, in the great age of liberalism, not merely institutions of learning that provided the rising generations of professional people with the instruction required for the satisfactory practice of their profession. They were centers of culture. Some of their teachers were known and admired all over the world. Their courses were attended not only by the regular students who planned to take academic degrees but by many mature men and women who were active in the professions, business, or politics, and expected from the lectures nothing but intellectual gratification. For instance, such outsiders, who were not students in a technical sense, thronged the courses in Paris of Renan, Fustel de Coulanges, and Bergson, and in Berlin those of Hegel, Helmholtz, Mommsen, and Treitschke. The educated public was seriously interested in the work of the academic circles. The elite read the books and the magazines published by the professors, joined their scholastic societies, and eagerly followed the discussions of the meetings.

Some of these amateurs who devoted only leisure hours to their studies rose high above the level of dilettantism. The history of modern science records the names of many such glorious "outsiders." It is, for instance, a characteristic fact that the only remarkable, although not epoch-making, contribution to economics that originated in the Germany of the second Reich came from a busy corporation counsel, Heinrich Oswalt from Frankfurt, a city that at the time his book was written had no university.[2]

In Vienna, also, close association of the university teachers with the cultured public of the city prevailed in the last decades of the nineteenth century and in the beginning of our century. It began to vanish when the old masters died or retired and men of smaller stature got their chairs. This was the period in which the rank of the Vienna University, as well as the cultural eminence of the city, was upheld and enlarged by a few of the *Privatdozents*. The outstanding case is that of psychoanalysis. It never got any encouragement from any official institution; it grew and thrived outside the university and its only connection with the bureaucratic hierarchy of learning was the fact that Freud was a *Privatdozent* with the meaningless title of professor.

There was in Vienna, as a heritage of the years in which the founders of the Austrian school had finally earned recognition, a lively interest in problems of economics. This interest enabled the present

---

[2] Cf. H. Oswalt, *Vortäge über wirtschaftliche Grundbegriffe,* 3rd ed. (Jena, 1920).

writer to organize a *Privatseminar* in the 1920s, to start the Economic Association, and to set up the Austrian Institute for Trade Cycle Research, that later changed its name to the Austrian Institute for Economic Research.

The *Privatseminar* had no connection whatever with the University or any other institution. Twice a month a group of scholars, among them several *Privatdozents,* met in the present writer's office in the Austrian Chamber of Commerce. Most of the participants belonged to the age group that had begun academic studies after the end of the first World War. Some were older. They were united by a burning interest in the whole field of the sciences of human action. In the debates, problems of philosophy, epistemology, economic theory, and the various branches of historical research were treated. The *Privatseminar* was discontinued when, in 1934, the present writer was appointed to the chair of international economic relations at the Graduate Institute of International Studies in Geneva, Switzerland.

With the exception of Richard von Strigl, whose early death put an untimely end to a brilliant scientific career, and Ludwig Bettelheim-Gabillon, about whom we will have more to say, all the members of the *Privatseminar* found a proper field for the continuation of their work as scholars, authors, and teachers outside of Austria.

In the realm of the spirit, Vienna played an eminent role in the years between the establishment of the Parliament in the early 1860s and the invasion of the Nazis in 1938. The flowering came suddenly after centuries of sterility and apathy. The decay had already begun many years before the Nazis intruded.

In all nations and in all periods of history, intellectual exploits were the work of a few men and were appreciated only by a small elite. The many looked upon these feats with hatred and disdain, at best with indifference. In Austria and in Vienna the elite were especially small, and the hatred of the masses and their leaders especially vitriolic.

4. Böhm-Bawerk and Wieser as Members of the Austrian Cabinet

The unpopularity of economics is the result of its analysis of the effects of privileges. It is impossible to invalidate the economists' demonstration that all privileges hurt the interests of the rest of the nation or at least of a great part of it, that those victimized will tolerate the existence of such privileges only if privileges are granted to them too, and then, when everybody is privileged, nobody wins but everybody loses on account of the resulting general drop in the productivity of labor.[3] However, the warnings of the economists are disregarded by the covetousness of people who are fully aware of their inability to succeed in a competitive market without the aid of special privileges. They are confident that they will get more valuable privileges than other groups or that they will be in a position to prevent, at least for some time, any granting of compensatory privileges to other groups. In their eyes the economist is simply a mischief-maker who wants to upset their plans.

When Menger, Böhm-Bawerk, and Wieser began their scientific careers, they were not concerned with the problems of economic policies and with the rejection of interventionism by Classical economics. They considered it as their vocation to put economic theory on a sound basis and they were ready to dedicate themselves entirely to this cause. Menger heartily disapproved of the interventionist policies that the Austrian government—like almost all governments of the epoch—had adopted. But he did not believe that he could contribute to a return to good policies in any other way than by expounding good economics in his books and articles as well as in his university teaching.

Böhm-Bawerk joined the staff of the Austrian Ministry of Finance in 1890. Twice he served for a short time as Minister of Finance in a caretaker cabinet. From 1900 to 1904 he was Minister of Finance in the cabinet headed by Ernest von Körber. Böhm's principles in the conduct of this office were strict maintenance of the legally fixed gold parity of the currency and a budget balanced without any aid from the central bank. An eminent scholar, Ludwig Bettelheim-Gabillon, planned to publish a comprehensive work analyzing Böhm-Bawerk's activity in the Ministry of France. Unfortunately the Nazis killed the author and destroyed his manuscript.[4]

Wieser was for some time during the first World War Minister of Commerce in the Austrian Cabinet. However, his activity was rather impeded by the far-reaching powers already given before Wieser took office to a functionary of the ministry, Richard Riedl. Virtually only matters of secondary importance were left to the jurisdiction of Wieser himself.

---

[3] *Cf.* Mises, *Human Action* (1949) and later editions, chapters XXVII-XXXVI.

[4] Only two chapters, which the author had published before the Anschluss, are preserved: "Böhm-Bawerk und die Brüsseler Zuckerkonvention" and "Böhm-Bawerk und die Konvertierung von Obligationen der einheitlichen Staatsschuld" in *Zeitschrift für Nationalökonomie*, Vol. VII and VIII (1936 and 1937).

II. The Conflict with the German Historical School

1. The German Rejection of Classical Economics

The hostility that the teachings of Classical economic theory encountered on the European continent was primarily caused by political prepossessions. Political economy as developed by several generations of English thinkers, brilliantly expounded by Hume and Adam Smith and perfected by Ricardo, was the most exquisite outcome of the philosophy of the Enlightenment. It was the gist of the liberal doctrine that aimed at the establishment of representative government and equality of all individuals under the law. It was not surprising that it was rejected by all those whose privileges it attacked. This propensity to spurn economics was considerably strengthened in Germany by the rising spirit of nationalism. The narrow-minded repudiation of Western civilization—philosophy, science, political doctrine and institutions, art and literature —which finally resulted in Nazism, originated in a passionate detraction of British political economy.

However, one must not forget that there were also other grounds for this revolt against political economy. This new branch of knowledge raised epistemological and philosophical problems for which the scholars did not find a satisfactory solution. It could not be integrated into the traditional system of epistemology and methodology. The empiricist tendency that dominates Western philosophy suggested considering economics as an experimental science like physics and biology. The very idea that a discipline dealing with "practical" problems like prices and wages could have an epistemological character different from that of other disciplines dealing with practical matters, was beyond the comprehension of the age. But on the other hand, only the most bigoted positivists failed to realize that experiments could not be performed in the field about which economics tries to provide knowledge.

We do not have to deal here with the state of affairs as it developed in the age of the neo-positivism or hyper-positivism of the twentieth century. Today, all over the world, but first of all in the United States, hosts of statisticians are busy in institutes devoted to what people believe is "economic research." They collect figures provided by governments and various business units, rearrange, readjust, and reprint them, compute averages and draw charts. They surmise that they are thereby "measuring" mankind's "behavior" and that there is no difference worth mentioning between their methods of investigation and those applied in the laboratories of physical, chemical, and biological research. They look with pity and contempt upon those economists who as they say, like the botanists of "antiquity," rely upon "much speculative thinking" instead of upon "experiments."[5] And they are fully convinced that out of their restless exertion there will one day emerge final and complete knowledge that will enable the planning authority of the future to make all people perfectly happy.

But with the economists of the first part of the nineteenth century, the misconstruction of the fundamentals of the sciences of human action did not yet go so far. Their attempts to deal with the epistemological problems of economics resulted, of course, in complete failure. Yet, in retrospect, we may say that this frustration was a necessary step on the way that led toward a more satisfactory solution of the problem. It was John Stuart Mill's abortive treatment of the methods of the moral sciences that unwittingly exposed the futility of all arguments advanced in favor of the empiricist interpretation of the nature of economics.

When Germans began to study the works of British Classical economics, they accepted without any qualms the assumption that economic theory is derived from experience. But this simple explanation could not satisfy those who disagreed with the conclusions which, from the Classical doctrine, had to be inferred for political action. They very soon raised questions: Is not the experience from which the British authors derived their theorems different from the experience which would have faced a German author? Is not British economics defective on account of the fact that the material of experience from which it is distilled was only Great Britain and only Great Britain of the Hanoverian Georges? Is there, after all, such a thing as an economic science valid for all countries, nations, and ages?

It is obvious how these three questions were answered by those who considered economics as an experimental discipline. But such an answer was tantamount to the apodictic negation of economics as such. The Historical school would have been consistent if it had rejected the very idea that such a thing as a science of economics is possible, and if it had scrupulously abstained from making any statements other than reports about what had happened at a definite moment of the past in a definite part of the earth. An anticipation of the effects to be expected from a definite event can be made only on the basis of a theory that claims general validity and not merely validity for what happened in the past in a definite country. The Historical school emphatically denied that there are economic theorems of such a universal validity.

---

[5] Cf. Arthur F. Burns, *The Frontiers of Economic Knowledge* (Princeton University Press, 1954), p. 189.

But this did not prevent them from recommending or rejecting—in the name of science—various opinions or measures necessarily designed to affect future conditions.

There was, e.g., the Classical doctrine concerning the effects of free trade and protection. The critics did not embark upon the (hopeless) task of discovering some false syllogisms in the chain of Ricardo's reasoning. They merely asserted that "absolute" solutions are not conceivable in such matters. There are historical situations, they said, in which the effects brought about by free trade or protection differ from those described by the "abstract" theory of "armchair" authors. To support their view they referred to various historical precedents. In doing this, they blithely neglected to consider that historical facts, being always the joint result of the operation of a multitude of factors, cannot prove or disprove any theorem.

Thus economics in the second German Reich, as represented by the government-appointed university professors, degenerated into an unsystematic, poorly assorted collection of various scraps of knowledge borrowed from history, geography, technology, jurisprudence, and party politics, larded with depreciatory remarks about the errors in the "abstractions" of the Classical school. Most of the professors more or less eagerly made propaganda in their writings and in their courses for the policies of the Imperial Government: authoritarian conservatism, *Sozialpolitik*, protectionism, huge armaments, and aggressive nationalism. It would be unfair to consider this intrusion of politics into the treatment of economics as a specifically German phenomenon. It was ultimately caused by the viciousness of the epistemological interpretation of economic theory, a failing that was not limited to Germany.

A second factor that made nineteenth-century Germany in general and especially the German universities look askance upon British political economy was its preoccupation with wealth and its relation to the utilitarian philosophy.

The then prevalent definitions of political economy described it as the science dealing with the production and distribution of wealth. Such a discipline could be nothing but despicable in the eyes of German professors. The professors thought of themselves as people self-denyingly engaged in the pursuit of pure knowledge and not, like the hosts of banausic money-makers, caring for earthly possessions. The mere mention of such base things as wealth and money was taboo among people boasting of their high culture (*Bildung*). The professors of economics could preserve their standing in the circles of their colleagues only by pointing out that the topic of their studies was not the mean concerns of profit-seeking business but historical research, e.g., about the lofty exploits of the Electors of Brandenburg and Kings of Prussia.

No less serious was the matter of utilitarianism. The utilitarian philosophy was not tolerated at German universities. Of the two outstanding German utilitarians, Ludwig Feuerbach never got any teaching job, while Rudolf von Jhering was a teacher of Roman Law. All the misunderstandings that for more than two thousand years have been advanced against Hedonism and Eudaemonism were rehashed by the professors of *Staatswissenschaften* in their criticisms of the British economists.[6] If nothing else had roused the suspicions of the German scholars, they would have condemned economics for the sole reason that Bentham and the Mills had contributed to it.

2. The Sterility of Germany in the Field of Economics

The German universities were owned and operated by the various kingdoms and grand duchies that formed the Reich.[7] The professors were civil servants and, as such, had to obey strictly the orders and regulations issued by their superiors, the bureaucrats of the ministries of public instruction. This total and unconditional subordination of the universities and their teachings to the supremacy of the governments was challenged—in vain—by German liberal public opinion when, in 1837, the King of Hanover fired seven professors of the University of Göttingen who protested against the King's breach of the constitution. The governments did not heed the public's reaction. They went on discharging professors with whose political or religious doctrines they did not agree. But after some time they resorted to more subtle and more efficacious methods to make the professors loyal supporters of the official policy. They scrupulously sifted the candidates before appointing them. Only reliable men got the chairs. Thus the question of academic freedom receded into the background. The professors of their own accord taught only what the government permitted them to teach.

The war of 1866 had ended the Prussian constitutional conflict. The King's party—the Conservative party of the Junkers, led by Bismarck—triumphed over the Prussian Progressive party that stood for parliamentary government, and likewise over the democratic groups of

---

[6] Later similar arguments were employed to discredit pragmatism. William James's dictum according to which the pragmatic method aims at bringing out of each word "its practical cash-value" (*Pragmatism*, 1907, p. 53) was quoted to characterize the meanness of the "dollar-philosophy."

[7] The Reich itself owned and operated only the University of Strassburg. The three German city-republics did not at that period have any university.

southern Germany. In the new political setting, first of the *Nord-deutscher Bund* and, after 1871, of the *Deutsches Reich,* there was no room left for the "alien" doctrines of Manchesterism and laissez faire. The victors of Königgrätz and Sedan thought they had nothing to learn from the "nation of shopkeepers"—the British—or from the defeated French.

At the outbreak of the war of 1870, one of the most eminent German scientists, Emil du Bois-Reymond, boasted that the University of Berlin was "the intellectual bodyguard of the House of Hohenzollern." This did not mean very much for the natural sciences, but it had a very clear and precise meaning for the sciences of human action. The incumbents of the chairs of history and of *Staatswissenschaften* (i.e., political science, including all things referring to economics and finance) knew what their sovereign expected of them. And they delivered the goods.

From 1882 to 1907 Friedrich Althoff was in the Prussian ministry of instruction in charge of university affairs. He ruled the Prussian universities as a dictator. As Prussia had the greatest number of lucrative professorships, and therefore offered the most favorable field for ambitious scholars, the professors in the other German states, nay even those of Austria and Switzerland, aspired to secure positions in Prussia. Thus Althoff could as a rule make them, too, virtually accept his principles and opinions. In all matters pertaining to the social sciences and the historical disciplines, Althoff entirely relied upon the advice of his friend Gustav von Schmoller. Schmoller had an unerring flair for separating the sheep from the goats.

In the second and third quarters of the nineteenth century some German professors wrote valuable contributions to economic theory. It is true that the most remarkable contributions of this period, those of Thünen and of Gossen, were not the work of professors but of men who did not hold teaching jobs. However, the books of Professors Hermann, Mangoldt, and Knies will be remembered in the history of economic thought. But after 1866, the men who came into the academic career had only contempt for "bloodless abstractions." They published historical studies, preferably such as dealt with labor conditions of the recent past. Many of them were firmly convinced that the foremost task of economists was to aid the "people" in the war of liberation they were waging against the "exploiters," and that the God-given leaders of the people were the dynasties, especially the Hohenzollern.

3. The Methodenstreit

In the *Untersuchungen* Menger rejected the epistemological ideas that underlay the writings of the Historical school. Schmoller published a rather contemptuous review of this book. Menger reacted, in 1884, with a pamphlet, *Die Irrtümer des Historismus in der Deutschen Nationalökonomie* [*The Errors of Historicism in German Economics*]. The various publications that this controversy engendered are known under the name of the *Methodenstreit,* the clash over methods.

The *Methodenstreit* contributed but little to the clarification of the problems involved. Menger was too much under the sway of John Stuart Mill's empiricism to carry his own point of view to its full logical consequences. Schmoller and his disciples, committed to defend an untenable position, did not even realize what the controversy was about.

The term *Methodenstreit* is, of course, misleading. For the issue was not to discover the most appropriate procedure for the treatment of the problems commonly considered as economic problems. The matter in dispute was essentially whether there could be such a thing as a science, other than history, dealing with aspects of human action.

There was, first of all, radical materialist determinism, a philosophy almost universally accepted in Germany at that time by physicists, chemists, and biologists, although it has never been expressly and clearly formulated. As these people saw it, human ideas, volitions, and actions are produced by physical and chemical events that the natural sciences will one day describe in the same way in which today they describe the emergence of a chemical compound out of the combination of several ingredients. As the only road that could lead to this final scientific accomplishment they advocated experimentation in physiological and biological laboratories.

Schmoller and his disciples passionately rejected this philosophy, not because they were aware of its deficiencies, but because it was incompatible with the religious tenets of the Prussian government. They virtually preferred to it a doctrine that was but little different from Comte's positivism, which, of course, they publicly disparaged on account of its atheism and its French origin. In fact, positivism, sensibly interpreted, must result in materialist determinism. But most of Comte's followers were not outspoken in this regard. Their discussions did not always preclude the conclusion that the laws of social physics (sociology), the establishment of which was in their opinion the highest goal of science, could be discovered by what they called a more "scientific" method of dealing with the material assembled by the traditional procedures of the historians. This was the position Schmoller embraced with regard to economics. Again and again he blamed the economists for having prematurely made inferences from quantitatively insufficient material. In his opinion, what was needed in order to substitute a realistic science of economics for the hasty generalizations of the British "armchair" economists was more statistics, more history, and more collection of "material." Out of the results of such research the economists of the future, he maintained, would one day develop new insights by "induction."

Schmoller was so confused that he failed to see the incompatibility of his own epistemological doctrine and the rejection of positivism's attack upon history. He did not realize the gulf that separated his views from those of the German philosophers who demolished positivism's ideas about the use and the treatment of history—first Dilthey, and later Windelband, Rickert, and Max Weber. In the same article in which he censured Menger's *Grundsätze*, he reviewed also the first important book of Dilthey, his *Einleitung in die Geisteswissenschaften*. But he did not grasp the fact that the tenor of Dilthey's doctrine was the annihilation of the fundamental thesis of his own epistemology, viz., that some laws of social development could be distilled from historical experience.

4. The Political Aspects of the Methodenstreit

The British free trade philosophy triumphed in the nineteenth century in the countries of western and central Europe. It demolished the shaky ideology of the authoritarian welfare state (*landesfürstlicher Wohlfahrtsstaat*) that had guided the policies of the German principalities in the eighteenth century. The culmination points of its free trade were the *Zollverein's* customs tariff of 1865 and the 1869 Trade Code (*Gewerbeordnung*) for the territory of the *Norddeutscher Bund* (later the *Deutsches Reich*). But very soon the government of Bismarck began to inaugurate its *Sozialpolitik,* the system of interventionist measures such as labor legislation, social security, pro-union attitudes, progressive taxation, protective tariffs, cartels, and dumping.[8]

If one tries to refute the devastating criticism leveled by economics against the suitability of all these interventionist schemes, one is forced to deny the very existence—not to mention the epistemological claims—of a science of economics, and of praxeology as well. This is what all the champions of authoritarianism, government omnipotence, and "welfare" policies have always done. They blame economics for being "abstract" and advocate a "visualizing" (*anschaulich*) mode of dealing with the problems involved. They emphasize that matters in this field are too complicated to be described in formulas and theorems. They assert that the various nations and races are so different from one

---

[8] *Cf.* Mises, *Omnipotent Government* (Yale University Press, 1944 and later editions), pp. 149ff.

another that their actions cannot be comprehended by a uniform theory; there are as many economic theories required as there are nations and races. Others add that even within the same nation or race, economic action is different in various epochs of history. These and similar objections, often incompatible with one another, are advanced in order to discredit economics as such.

In fact, economics disappeared entirely from the universities of the German Empire. There was a lone epigone of Classical economics left at the University of Bonn, Heinrich Dietzel, who, however, never understood what the theory of subjective value meant. At all other universities the teachers were anxious to ridicule economics and the economists. It is not worthwhile to dwell upon the stuff that was handed down as a substitute for economics at Berlin, Munich, and other universities of the Reich. Nobody cares today about all that Gustav von Schmoller, Adolph Wagner, Lujo Brentano, and their numerous adepts wrote in their voluminous books and magazines.

The political significance of the work of the Historical school consisted in the fact that it rendered Germany safe for the ideas, the acceptance of which made popular with the German people all those disastrous policies that resulted in the great catastrophes. The aggressive imperialism that twice ended in war and defeat, the limitless inflation of the early 1920s, the *Zwangswirtschaft* [command economy] and all the horrors of the Nazi regime were achievements of politicians who acted as they had been taught by the champions of the Historical school.

Schmoller and his friends and disciples advocated what has been called state socialism; i.e., a system of socialism—planning—in which the top management would be in the hands of the Junker aristocracy. It was this brand of socialism at which Bismarck and his successors were aiming. The timid opposition which they encountered on the part of a small group of businessmen was negligible, not so much on account of the fact that these opponents were not numerous, but because their endeavors lacked any ideological backing. There were no longer any liberal thinkers left in Germany. The only resistance that was offered to the party of state socialism came from the Marxian party of the Social-Democrats. Like the Schmoller socialists—the socialists of the chair (*Kathedersozialisten*)—the Marxists advocated socialism. The only difference between the two groups was in the choice of the people who should operate the supreme planning board: the Junkers, the professors, and the bureaucracy of Hohenzollern Prussia, or the officers of the Social-Democratic party and their affiliated labor unions.

Thus the only serious adversaries whom the Schmoller school had to fight in Germany were the Marxists. In this controversy the latter very soon got the upper hand. For they at least had a body of doctrine, however faulty and contradictory it was, while the teachings of the Historical school were rather the denial of any theory. In search of a modicum of theoretical support, the Schmoller school step by step began to borrow from the spiritual fund of the Marxists. Finally, Schmoller himself largely endorsed the Marxian doctrine of class conflict and of the "ideological" impregnation of thought by the thinker's class membership. One of his friends and fellow professors, Wilhelm Lexis, developed a theory of interest that Engels characterized as a paraphrase of the Marxian theory of exploitation.[9] It was an effect of the writings of the champions of the *Sozialpolitik* that the epithet "bourgeois" (*bürgerlich*) acquired in the German language an opprobrious connotation.

The crushing defeat in the first World War shattered the prestige of the German princes, aristocrats, and bureaucrats. The adepts of the Historical school and *Sozialpolitik* transferred their loyalty to various splinter-groups, out of which the German Nationalist-Socialist Workers' Party, the Nazis, eventually emerged.

The straight line that leads from the work of the Historical school to Nazism cannot be shown in sketching the evolution of one of the founders of the school, for the protagonists of the *Methodenstreit* era had finished the course of their lives before the defeat of 1918 and the rise of Hitler. But the life of the outstanding man among the school's second generation illustrates all the phases of German university economics in the period from Bismarck to Hitler.

Werner Sombart was by far the most gifted of Schmoller's students. He was only twenty-five when his master, at the height of the *Methodenstreit*, entrusted him with the job of reviewing and annihilating Wieser's book, *Der natürliche Wert*. The faithful disciple condemned the book as "entirely unsound."[10] Twenty years later Sombart boasted that he had dedicated a good part of his life to fighting for Marx.[11] When the War broke out in 1914, Sombart published a book, *Händler und Helden* [Hucksters and Heroes].[12] There, in uncouth and foul language, he rejected everything British or Anglo-Saxon, but above all British philosophy and economics, as a manifestation of a mean jobber mentality. After the War, Sombart revised his book on socialism. Before the War it

---

[9] *Cf.* the more detailed analysis in Mises, *Kritik des Interventionismus* (Jena, 1929), pp. 92 ff. [English translation: *Critique of Interventionism* (Arlington House, 1977), pp. 108ff.]

[10] *Cf. Schmoller's Jahrbuch*, Vol. 13 (1889), pp. 1488–1490.

[11] *Cf.* Sombart, *Das Lebenswerk von Karl Marx* (Jena, 1909), p. 3.

[12] *Cf.* Sombart, *Händler und Helden* (Munich, 1915).

had been published in nine editions.[13] While the pre-war editions had praised Marxism, the tenth edition fanatically attacked it, especially on account of its "proletarian" character and its lack of patriotism and nationalism. A few years later Sombart tried to revive the *Methodenstreit* by a volume full of invectives against economists whose thought he was unable to understand.[14] Then when the Nazis seized power, he crowned a literary career of forty-five years by a book on German Socialism. The guiding idea of this work was that the *Führer* gets his orders from God, the supreme *Führer* of the universe, and that *Führertum* is a permanent revelation.[15]

Such was the progress of German academic economics from Schmoller's glorification of the Hohenzollern Electors and Kings to Sombart's canonization of Adolf Hitler.

5. The Liberalism of the Austrian Economists

Plato dreamed of the benevolent tyrant who would entrust the wise philosopher with the power to establish the perfect social system. The Enlightenment did not put its hopes upon the more or less accidental emergence of well-intentioned rulers and provident sages. Its optimism concerning mankind's future was founded upon the double faith in the goodness of man and in his rational mind. In the past a minority of villains—crooked kings, sacrilegious priests, corrupt noblemen—were able to make mischief. But now—according to Enlightenment doctrine—as man has become aware of the power of his reason, a relapse into the darkness and failings of ages gone by is no longer to be feared. Every new generation will add something to the good accomplished by its ancestors. Thus mankind is on the eve of a continuous advance toward more satisfactory conditions. To progress steadily is the nature of man. It is vain to complain about the alleged lost bliss of a fabulous golden age. The ideal state of society is before us, not behind us.

Most of the nineteenth-century liberal, progressive, and democratic politicians who advocated representative government and universal suffrage were guided by a firm confidence in the infallibility of the common man's rational mind. In their eyes majorities could not err.

---

[13] *Cf.* Sombart, *Der proletarische Sozialismus*, 10th ed. (Jena, 1924), 2 vol.

[14] *Cf.* Sombart, *Die drei Nationalökonomien* (Munich, 1930).

[15] *Cf.* Sombart, *Deutscher Sozialismus* (Charlottenburg, 1934), p. 213. (In the American edition: *A New Social Philosophy*, translated and edited by K. F. Geiser, Princeton, 1937, p. 149.) Sombart's achievements were appreciated abroad. Thus, e.g., in 1929 he was elected to honorary membership in the American Economic Association.

Ideas that originated from the people and were approved by the voters could not but be beneficial to the commonweal.

It is important to realize that the arguments brought forward in favor of representative government by the small group of liberal philosophers were quite different and did not imply any reference to an alleged infallibility of majorities. Hume had pointed out that government is always founded upon opinion. In the long run the opinion of the many always wins out. A government that is not supported by the opinion of the majority must sooner or later lose its power; if it does not abdicate, it is violently overthrown by the many. Peoples have the power eventually to put those men at the helm who are prepared to rule according to the principles that the majority considers adequate. There is, in the long run, no such thing as an unpopular government maintaining a system that the multitude condemns as unfair. The rationale of representative government is not that majorities are God-like and infallible; it is the intent to bring about by peaceful methods the ultimately unavoidable adjustment of the political system and the men operating its steering mechanism to the ideology of the majority. The horrors of revolution and civil war can be avoided if a disliked government can be smoothly dislodged at the next election.

The true liberals firmly held that the market economy, the only economic system that warrants a steadily progressing improvement of mankind's material welfare, can work only in an atmosphere of undisturbed peace. They advocated government by the people's elected representatives because they took it for granted that only this system will lastingly preserve peace both in domestic and in foreign affairs.

What separated these true liberals from the blind majority-worship of the self-styled radicals was that they based their optimism concerning mankind's future not upon the mystic confidence in the infallibility of majorities but upon the belief that the power of sound logical argument is irresistible. They did not fail to see that the immense majority of common men are both too dull and too indolent to follow and to absorb long chains of reasoning. But they hoped that these masses, precisely on account of their dullness and indolence, could not help endorsing the ideas that the intellectuals brought to them. From the sound judgment of the cultured minority and from their ability to persuade the majority, the great leaders of the nineteenth-century liberal movement expected the steady improvement of human affairs.

In this regard there was full agreement between Carl Menger and his two earliest followers, Wieser and Böhm-Bawerk. Among the unpublished papers of Menger, Professor Hayek discovered a note that reads: "There is no better means to disclose the absurdity of a mode of reasoning than to let it pursue its full course to the end." All three of them liked to refer to Spinoza's argumentation in the first book of his *Ethics* that ends in the famous dictum, "*Sane sicut lux se ipsam et tenebras manifestat, sic veritas norma sui et falsi*" ["Indeed, just as light defines itself and darkness, so truth sets the standard for itself and falsity"]. They looked calmly upon the passionate propaganda of both the Historical school and Marxism. They were fully convinced that the logically indefensible dogmas of these factions would eventually be rejected by all reasonable men precisely on account of their absurdity and that the masses of common men would necessarily follow the lead of the intellectuals.[16]

The wisdom of this mode of arguing is to be seen in the avoidance of the popular practice of playing off an alleged psychology against logical reasoning. It is true that often errors in reasoning are caused by the individual's disposition to prefer an erroneous conclusion to the correct one. There are even hosts of people whose affections simply prevent them from straight thinking. But it is a far cry from the establishment of these facts to the doctrines that in the last generation were taught under the label "sociology of knowledge." Human thinking and reasoning, human science and technology are the product of a social process insofar as the individual thinker faces both the achievements and the errors of his predecessors and enters into a virtual discussion with them either in assenting or dissenting. It is possible for the history of ideas to make understandable a man's failings as well as his exploits by analyzing the conditions under which he lived and worked. In this sense only is it permissible to refer to what is called the spirit of an age, a nation, a milieu. But it is circular reasoning if one tries to explain the emergence of an idea, still less to justify it, by referring to its author's environment. Ideas always spring from the mind of an individual, and history cannot say anything more about them than that they were generated at a definite instant of time by a definite individual. There is no other excuse for a man's erroneous thinking than what an Austrian government once declared with regard to the case of a defeated general—that nobody is answerable for not being a genius. Psychology may help us to explain why a man failed in his thinking. But no such explanation can convert what is false into truth.

The Austrian economists unconditionally rejected the logical relativism implied in the teachings of the Prussian or German Historical

---

[16] There is need to add that Menger, Böhm-Bawerk, and Wieser looked with the utmost pessimism upon the political future of the Austrian Empire. But this problem cannot be dealt with in this essay.

school. As against the declarations of Schmoller and his followers, they maintained that there is a body of economic theorems that are valid for all human action irrespective of time and place, the national and racial characteristics of the actors, and their religious, philosophical, and ethical ideologies.

The greatness of the service these three Austrian economists have rendered by maintaining the cause of economics against the vain critique of Historicism cannot be overrated. They did not infer from their epistemological convictions any optimism concerning mankind's future evolution. Whatever is to be said in favor of correct logical thinking does not prove that the coming generations of men will surpass their ancestors in intellectual effort and achievements. History shows that again and again periods of marvelous mental accomplishments were followed by periods of decay and retrogression. We do not know whether the next generation will beget people who are able to continue along the lines of the geniuses who made the last centuries so glorious. We do not know anything about the biological conditions that enable a man to make one step forward in the march of intellectual advancement. We cannot preclude the assumption that there may be limits to man's further intellectual ascent. And certainly we do not know whether in this ascent there is not a point beyond which the intellectual leaders can no longer succeed in convincing the masses and making them follow their lead.

The inference drawn from these premises by the Austrian economists was that, while it is the duty of a pioneering mind to do all that his faculties enable him to perform, it is not incumbent upon him to propagandize for his ideas, still less to use questionable methods in order to make his thoughts palatable to people. They were not concerned about the circulation of their writings. Menger did not publish a second edition of his famous *Grundsätze,* although the book was long since out of print, second-hand copies sold at high prices, and the publisher urged him again and again to consent.

The main and only concern of the Austrian economists was to contribute to the advancement of economics. They never tried to win the support of anybody by other means than by the convincing power developed in their books and articles. They looked with indifference upon the fact that the universities of the German-speaking countries, even many of the Austrian universities, were hostile to economics as such and still more so to the new economic doctrines of subjectivism.

III. The Place of the Austrian School of Economics in the Evolution of Economics

1. The "Austrian School" and Austria

When the German professors attached the epithet "Austrian" to the theories of Menger and his two earliest followers and continuators, they meant it in a pejorative sense. After the battle of Königgrätz—1866, when the Prussians under William I roundly defeated the Austrian army—the qualification of a thing as Austrian always had such a derogatory coloration in Berlin, that "headquarters of *Geist*" as Herbert Spencer sneeringly called it.[17] But the intended smear boomeranged. Very soon the designation "The Austrian School" was famous all over the world.

Of course, the practice of attaching a national label to a line of thought is necessarily misleading. Only very few Austrians—and for that matter, non-Austrians—knew anything about economics, and still smaller was the number of those Austrians whom one could call economists, however generous one might be in conferring this appellation. Besides, there were among the Austrian-born economists some who did not work along the lines which were called the "Austrian School." Best known among them were the mathematicians Rudolf Auspitz and Richard Lieben, and later Alfred Amonn and Josef Schumpeter. On the other hand, the number of foreign economists who applied themselves to the continuation of the work inaugurated by the "Austrians" was steadily increasing. At the beginning it sometimes happened that the endeavors of these British, American, and other non-Austrian economists met with opposition in their own countries and that they were ironically called "Austrians" by their critics. But after some years all the essential ideas of the Austrian school were by and large accepted as an integral part of economic theory. About the time of Menger's demise (1921), one no longer distinguished been an Austrian school and other economics. The appellation "Austrian School" became the name given to an important chapter of the history of economic thought; it was no longer the name of a specific sect with doctrines different from those held by other economists.

There was, of course, one exception. The interpretation of the causes and the course of the trade cycle which the present writer provided, first in his *Theory of Money and Credit*[18] and finally in his treatise

---

[17] *Cf.* Herbert Spencer, *The Study of Sociology,* 9th edition (London, 1880), p. 217.

[18] German-language editions, 1912 and 1924, English-language editions 1934, 1953 [1980].

Human Action [19] under the name of the Monetary or Circulation Credit Theory of the trade cycle, was called by some authors the Austrian theory of the trade cycle. Like all such national labels, this too is objectionable. The Circulation Credit Theory is a continuation, enlargement, and generalization of ideas first developed by the British Currency School and of some additions to them made by later economists, among them also the Swede, Knut Wicksell.

As it has been unavoidable to refer to the national label, "the Austrian School," one may add a few words about the linguistic group to which the Austrian economists belonged. Menger, Böhm-Bawerk, and Wieser were German Austrians; their language was German and they wrote their books in German. The same is true of their most eminent students—Johann von Komorzynski, Hans Mayer, Robert Meyer, Richard Schüller, Richard von Strigl, and Robert Zuckerkandl. In this sense the work of the Austrian school is an accomplishment of German philosophy and science. But among the students of Menger, Böhm-Bawerk, and Wieser there were also non-German Austrians. Two of them have distinguished themselves by eminent contributions, the Czechs Franz Čuhel and Karel Engliš.

2. The Historical Significance of the Methodenstreit

The peculiar state of German ideological and political conditions in the last quarter of the nineteenth century generated the conflict between two schools of thought out of which the *Methodenstreit* and the appellation "Austrian School" emerged. But the antagonism that manifested itself in this debate is not confined to a definite period or country. It is perennial. As human nature is, it is unavoidable in any society where the division of labor and its corollary, market exchange, have reached such an intensity that everybody's subsistence depends on other people's conduct. In such a society everybody is served by his fellow men, and in turn, he serves them. The services are rendered voluntarily: in order to make a fellow do something for me, I have to offer him something which he prefers to abstention from doing that something. The whole system is built upon this voluntariness of the services exchanged. Inexorable natural conditions prevent man from indulging in a carefree enjoyment of his existence. But his integration into the community of the market economy is spontaneous, the result of the insight that there is no better or, for that matter, no other method of survival open to him.

---

[19] First edition, Yale University Press, 1949; 4th edition, Foundation for Economic Education, 1996.

However, the meaning and bearing of this spontaneousness are only grasped by economists. All those not familiar with economics, i.e., the immense majority, do not see any reason why they should not coerce other people by means of force to do what these people are not prepared to do of their own accord. Whether this apparatus of physical compulsion resorted to in such endeavors is that of the government's police power or an illegal "picket" force whose violence the government tolerates, does not make any difference. What matters is the substitution of compulsion for voluntary action.

Due to a definite constellation of political conditions that could be called accidental, the rejection of the philosophy of peaceful cooperation was, in modern times, first developed into a comprehensive doctrine by subjects of the Prussian State. The victories in the three Bismarck wars had intoxicated the German scholars, most of whom were servants of the government. Some people considered it a characteristic fact that the adoption of the ideas of the Schmoller school was slowest in the countries whose armies had been defeated in 1866 and 1870. It is, of course, preposterous to search for any connection between the rise of the Austrian economic theory and the defeats, failures, and frustrations of the Habsburg regime. Yet, the fact that the French state universities kept out of the way of historicism and *Sozialpolitik* longer than those of other nations was certainly, at least to some extent, caused by the Prussian label attached to these doctrines. France, like all other countries, became a stronghold of interventionism and proscribed economics.

The philosophical consummation of the ideas glorifying the government's interference, i.e., the action of the armed constables, was achieved by Nietzsche and by Georges Sorel. They coined most of the slogans that guided the butcheries of Bolshevism, Fascism, and Nazism. Intellectuals extolling the delights of murder, writers advocating censorship, philosophers judging the merits of thinkers and authors, not according to the value of their contributions but according to their achievements on battlefields,[20] are the spiritual leaders of our age of perpetual strife. What a spectacle was offered by those American authors and professors who ascribed the origin of their own nation's political independence and constitution to a clever trick of the "special interests," while casting longing glances at the Soviet paradise of Russia!

The greatness of the nineteenth century consisted in the fact that to some extent the ideas of Classical economics became the dominant phi-

---

[20] *Cf.* the passages quoted by Julien Benda, *La trahison des clercs* (Paris, 1927), Appendix, Note O, pp. 292–295 [English translation, *The Betrayal of the Intellectuals.* Boston: Beacon Press, 1955. ed.]

losophy of state and society. They transformed the traditional status society into nations of free citizens, royal absolutism into representative government, and above all, the poverty of the masses under the *ancien régime* into the well-being of the many under capitalistic laissez faire. Today the reaction of statism and socialism is sapping the foundations of Western civilization and well-being. Perhaps those are right who assert that it is too late to prevent the final triumph of barbarism and destruction. However this may be, one thing is certain—society, i.e., peaceful cooperation of men under the principle of the division of labor, can exist and work only if it adopts policies that economic analysis declares as fit for attaining the ends sought. The worst illusion of our age is the superstitious confidence placed in panaceas which—as the economists have irrefutably demonstrated—are contrary to purpose.

Governments, political parties, pressure groups, and the bureaucrats of the educational hierarchy think they can avoid the inevitable consequences of unsuitable measures by boycotting and silencing the independent economists. But truth persists and works, even if nobody is left to utter it.

Austrian School of Economics*

by Ludwig von Mises

Usually when referring to economics in Vienna and Austria, one speaks of the "Austrian School." Many people misunderstand this term, believing there was a special Austrian school of economics in Vienna, an organized institution like a law school in this country. Now the fact is that the term "school" in connection with Austrian economics refers to a certain trend in doctrines; it is a doctrinal term.

The term "Austrian School" was originally given to a small group of Austrian economists by their adversaries in Germany. When the term was first used against the Austrians in the 1880s, it was used as a pejorative, with a certain amount of contempt. In this respect, it differed greatly from the names of the other two Austrian groups—the Psycho-analytical Movement and the Vienna Circle of Logical Positivism, both of which chose their names themselves. Both these other two groups have become internationally known as scientific groups. As a matter of fact, the so-called Logical Positivists have come to dominate the teaching of philosophy in the Anglo-Saxon universities, first of all in England and in the United States, not so much in France. What all these three groups had in common is that they were not very popular with the authorities of the official Austrian academic hierarchy.

All the universities in Continental Europe are state universities. Even the idea that a university could be a private institution is foreign to most of these countries. So the universities are operated by the government. But there was a fundamental difference between them and other governmental institutions; the difference was that the professors enjoyed academic freedom.

All government employees, functionaries of the government, are bound, in the exercise of their functions, to obey strictly what they have been told and ordered to do by their supervisors. But although the teachers at the universities, technological universities, and all other schools of the same rank, were government employees, they had no

* Address at New York University Faculty Club, May 2, 1962. Dr. Mises was introduced by Dr. William H. Peterson, then a professor at New York University Graduate School of Business Administration. In the audience was Friedrich A. Hayek, professor of social and moral science of the Committee on Social Thought at the University of Chicago.

superiors; they enjoyed academic freedom. Nobody, not even a member of the cabinet supervising the duties of the supreme management of instruction, had the right to interfere in any way with their teaching. This was of very great importance because the tendency has prevailed again and again for the government in these countries to influence the teaching of law, also of economics, political science, and the social sciences in general.

Now the important fact was that these three groups—the Austrian School of Economics, the Vienna School of Logical Positivism, and the Psychoanalytical Movement—had one thing in common. In the postwar period, at least, they were represented, not by professors appointed to teach, but by *Privatdozents*. A *Privatdozent* is an institution unknown to the universities of the Anglo-Saxon countries. A *Privatdozent* is a man who is admitted as a private teacher at the university. He does not receive any payment from the government; actually he has only the very unimportant right to receive the fees paid by his students. Most *Privatdozents* made the equivalent from their fees of about $5.00 or $10.00 a year. Therefore they had to find some other means of making a living in whatever way they wanted. As for me I served as economic adviser to the Austrian government's Chamber of Commerce.

I had been admitted to lecture at the University of Vienna as a *Privatdozent* a little over a year before the outbreak of the first World War. The War interrupted my teaching. When I came back from the War many years later, I found that many young men were very much interested in the study of economics; they wanted not only to pass the examinations but to become economists and contribute something to teaching and research in the field.

In regard to the study of modern languages the preparation of students in Austria for economics and legal studies, which were combined at the university, was very unsatisfactory. Instruction was rather good in Greek and Latin at the lower level of the Austrian Gymnasium [high school/junior college], as well as at the Gymnasiums of other European countries, say in France and Germany, but modern languages were neglected. Those who knew French and English had acquired their knowledge privately, which was not so easy to do during the War. And after the War the young men, who came to the seminar that I conducted as a *Privatdozent,* were practically not at all familiar with any foreign language. One of these men, Fritz Machlup, now a professor at one of the best known and biggest American universities, Princeton, tells me every time we meet, "Do you remember you gave me a list of books for a paper I had to prepare for your seminar, and on this list English-language books dominated?" Dismayed, Machlup had told me, "But these are English books!" Machlup reminds me I had then answered, "Certainly. Learn English."

Already at that time, immediately after the war, I had my first American student. This American student came to Vienna, not as a private citizen, but as a lieutenant in the U.S. army, as the aide-de-camp to another American, an older man, a colonel. The colonel's assignment in Vienna gave him practically nothing to do so he had a lot of leisure time. His young assistant had still less to do, and still more leisure time. He decided to use his leisure time in a way that would make it possible for him to take back to the United States with him, to Harvard University, a ready-made doctoral dissertation. In my seminar he wrote a doctoral dissertation on direct taxation in Austria. In the United States the income tax was at that time very new. Austria, with its 100-year history of income taxes and its corporation tax, had far more experience than the United States, so there was a lot for Americans to learn from Austria about taxes. This young man, John Van Sickle, became a very well known author of books and is today a retired professor of Wabash College.

I had a two-hour seminar once a week at the University. But very soon that appeared insufficient. There were students in the seminar who had already acquired a very good knowledge of economic problems and who wanted to do serious research work. And then there were beginning students. So very soon I started a *Privatseminar*, which is considered by the German, French, and Austrian systems to be the most important work a professor can do. A *Privatseminar* has practically no official or legal connection with the university; it is simply an institution which permits a member of the faculty to meet regularly with his students to work and discuss problems of economics and history.

Now I started such a *Privatseminar*, and I must say that, looking back today, this *Privatseminar* was a success. In this very room I see one of its earliest members, Professor Hayek. And there are others from my seminar who are now teaching in this country—Gottfried Haberler at Harvard, Fritz Machlup and Oskar Morgenstern at Princeton. At Marquette University, there is Walter Froelich. Then there is a lady, Dr. Ilse Mintz, professor at Columbia University's School of General Studies.

We dealt with all kinds of problems which related economics to the other social sciences, for there were not only economists in my *Privatseminar*. Many of the students were less interested in economics as such than in the general problems of the social sciences and the sciences of human action. One of these was Eric Voegelin, for 20 years professor at

Louisiana State University, Baton Rouge, and now Professor of Philosophy at the University of Munich in Germany. Voegelin's name may perhaps be known to you as he acquired some fame as an author of philosophical books. Then there were two professors who taught at the New School for Social Research, Dr. Alfred Schütz and Dr. Felix Kaufmann. You will be perhaps astonished to learn that one member of my seminar, Dr. Emanuel Winternitz, teaches, or taught, history of art at Yale. You may be still more astonished to hear that Dr. Winternitz was a practicing lawyer and that when he came to this country he was almost immediately appointed by the Metropolitan Museum to a position in his specialty, a very special field dealing with problems in which painting and music come together; he is now head of one of the departments of the Metropolitan Museum of Art.

There were others, foreigners who came to Vienna for a time and attended my seminar, not very regularly but often enough. I shall mention only a few. As you know I am not very much in favor of Marxism and similar doctrines, so you will be astonished to hear that one of these foreigners was Hugh Gaitskell, the present chief of the British Labor Party. Again you will be astonished to learn that another was a Japanese professor, Kotari Araki, who, later as a professor at the University of Berlin during the time of the Axis, taught about Japanese economics and Axis economic problems. I want to mention one other foreigner who attended my seminar, François Perroux, the present professor of economics at the Collège de France, the most renowned institution of French learning. There were also many others.

Due to the inflation and the economic conditions in Europe at that time, the problem for European students in general and for young students in Austria in particular was to a great extent financial. The regular study of economics was rather difficult for persons who couldn't afford to buy texts and other books, especially as libraries, even the official libraries, didn't have the money to buy them either. Therefore, it was of very great importance to find the means and the method to give these young men an opportunity to go abroad.

The first student of mine who went to a foreign country in this way was Professor Hayek. A distinguished professor at New York University, Jeremiah Jenks, who had written important studies on the gold exchange standard in the Far East; one could say that Jenks was the man who made the gold exchange standard known to economists. Jenks came to Vienna because he wanted to study and write about European conditions and I introduced him to Hayek. Later by special arrangement, Dr. Hayek became Jenks' secretary for some time in New York. This was an exceptional case. Both Jeremiah Jenks and Hayek were exceptional men. To help others, it was necessary to find some other way.

One American institution that did an excellent job in this regard was the Laura Spelman Foundation, better known as the Rockefeller Foundation. Laura Spelman was the wife of the original old Rockefeller. This Laura Spelman Foundation made it possible for young European scholars to spend one or two years in the United States. They could attend universities if they wanted and visit different parts of the country; they could really derive great advantages from the arrangement.

The man who represented the Foundation in Austria was a professor of history, Francis Pribram. Pribram also accepted economists whom I recommended, and in the course of the years Gottfried Haberler, Oskar Morgenstern, Fritz Machlup, and several others came to the United States, spent two years here under the Foundation's auspices, and then went back as, I would say, "perfect" economists. As you know, they later wrote many very interesting and good books. One other Laura Spelman student I might mention was the German, Professor Wilhelm Roepke.

Another thing that developed out of my *Privatseminar* and my activities as economic adviser to the Austrian Chamber of Commerce was that in 1926 in Vienna we started the Institute for Business Cycle Research. Its first manager was again Professor Hayek. When Hayek left Vienna in 1931 to teach at the London School of Economics, Morgenstern, now professor at Princeton, succeeded him. In spite of some "unpleasant" experiences with the Nazis, this Institute still exists in Austria, although it is no longer the Institute for Business Cycle Research but a more general institute, the Austrian Institute for Economic Research.

What is very interesting is that these students, who studied in the 1920s at the Austrian universities and wanted to choose a scientific career and contribute to the development of science, let us say, as researchers in economics, had at that time in Austria very slim chances of making sufficient money or earning a living in this capacity. As students they knew very well that they would have to work in some other field and would only be able to devote their leisure time to their true interest, the study of economics. At that time they couldn't know that, when Austria was invaded by Nazi Germany in 1938, many of them would be able to find teaching positions in foreign countries, especially here in the United States, and that they would find here a much broader field of activity than any they could ever have found in Austria.

Therefore, I must say that I consider the real success of my work as a professor of economics in Vienna was that I made it possible for a number of very gifted and able men to find a way to devote their lives to scientific research. This, of course, was not due to my merit. It was something that developed because of the general attitude in this country that accepted these young European refugees as teachers without regard to the fact that they were not born Americans and that they had been educated and had reached maturity in Europe under very different situations. What this country gained from these former students of mine is not bad; certainly today they now hold very good positions. As teachers of economics in this country, they have contributed to the success of American universities and especially to the departments of the social sciences and economics. Many are also working in other fields and in branches of business, often academic businesses.

There is a lot of talk today about international cooperation and international friendship among nations. In fact, nothing has been done officially in this regard. On the contrary the world is still divided in hostile camps, which is very unfortunate. But what has really developed unofficially in the world is an internationalism of science and teaching. I am proud that I could contribute a little bit to this internationalization. The fact that today there is international cooperation among members of the same field of research is one of the most important developments of recent years. We can all be proud of the fact that we have contributed a little bit to its development.

EPISTEMOLOGY

The Austrian Economists[1]

by Eugen von Böhm-Bawerk

The editors of this magazine have requested from my pen an account of the work of that group of economists which is popularly called the "Austrian School." Since I am myself a member of the group, possibly I shall prove to be no impartial expositor. I will, nevertheless, comply with the request as well as I can, and I will attempt to describe what we Austrians are actually doing and seeking to do.

The Most Important Doctrines of Classical Economists Are No Longer Tenable

The province of the Austrian economists is *theory* in the strict sense of the word. They are of the opinion that the theoretical part of political economy needs to be thoroughly transformed. The most important and most famous doctrines of the Classical economists are either no longer tenable at all, or are tenable only after essential alterations and additions. In the conviction of the inadequacy of the Classical political economy, the Austrian economists and the adherents of the Historical school agree. But in regard to the final cause of the inadequacy, there is a fundamental difference of opinion which has led to a lively contention over methods.

The Historical school believes the ultimate source of the errors of the Classical economy to be the false method by which it was pursued. It was almost entirely abstract-deductive, and, in their opinion, political economy should be only, or at least chiefly, inductive. In order to accomplish the necessary reform of the science, we must change the method of investigation; we must abandon abstraction and set ourselves to collecting empirical material—devote ourselves to history and statistics.

---

[1] Originally published in *The Annals* of the American Academy of Political Science, January 1891; translated by Henrietta Leonard; reprinted here from *Shorter Classics of Eugen von Böhm-Bawerk,* Vol. 1, with the permission of the publisher, Libertarian Press.

The Austrians, Although Primarily Interested in Theory, Have Been Obliged to Defend Their Views on Method

The Austrians, on the contrary, are of the opinion that the errors of the Classical economists were only, so to speak, the ordinary diseases of the childhood of the science. Political economy is even yet one of the youngest sciences, and it was still younger in the time of Classical economics which, in spite of its name "Classical," given as the event proved too soon, was only an incipient, embryonic science. It has never happened in any other case that the whole of a science was discovered at the first attempt, even by the greatest genius, and so it is not surprising that the whole of political economy was not discovered, even by the Classical school. Their greatest fault was that they were forerunners; our greatest advantage is that we come after. We who are richer by the fruits of a century's research than were our predecessors, need not work by different methods, but simply work better than they. The Historical school are certainly right in holding that our theories should be supported by as abundant empirical material as possible; but they are wrong in giving to the work of data collection an abnormal preference, and in wishing either entirely to dispense with, or at least to push into the background, the use of abstract generalization. Without such generalization there can be no science at all.

Numerous works of the Austrian economists are devoted to this strife over methods;[2] among them the *Untersuchungen über die Methode der Sozialwissenschaften*, by C. Menger, stands first in deep and exhaus-

---

[2] Menger, *Untersuchungen über die Methode der Sozialwissenschaften*, 1883. [The original German-language text was republished in *Collected Works of Carl Menger*, Vol. II, London School of Economics and Political Science, University of London, 1933 (Reprint No. 18).] English translation, *Problems of Economics and Sociology* (Urbana, Ill.: University of Illinois Press, 1963; reprinted as *Investigations into the Method of the Social Sciences*, New York: New York University Press, 1985; Grove City, Pa.: Libertarian Press, 1996).

Menger, *Die Irrtümer des Historismus in der deutschen Nationalökonomie, 1884.* [Republished in "Kleinere Schriften zur Methode und Geschichte der Volkswirtschaftslehre," *Collected Works of Carl Menger*, Vol. III, London School of Economics and Political Science, 1938 (Reprint No. 19).]

Menger, "Grundzüge einer Klassifikation der Wirtschaftswissenschaften," in Conrad's *Jahrbuch für Nationalökonomie und Statistik*, N. F., Vol. XIX, 1889. [Republished in "Kleinere Schriften zur Methode und Geschichte der Volkswirtschaftslehre," *Collected Works of Carl Menger*, Vol. III, London School of Economics and Political Science, 1935 (Reprint No. 19). English translation by Louise Sommer, "Toward A Systematic Classification of the Economic Sciences," Chapter I, *Essays in European Economic Thought*, Princeton, N.J.: D. Van Nostrand, 1960.]

Sax, *Das Wesen und die Aufgabe der Nationalökonomie*, 1884.

Phillippovich, *Über Aufgabe und Methode der politischen Ökonomie*, 1886.

tive treatment of the problems involved. It should be noticed in this connection that the "exact" or, as I prefer to call it, the "isolating" method recommended by Menger, together with the "empirico-realist" method, is by no means purely speculative or unempirical but, on the contrary, seeks and always finds its foundation in experience. But although the strife of methods, perhaps more than anything else, has drawn attention to the Austrian economists, I prefer to regard it as an unimportant episode of their activity. The matter of importance to them was, and is, the reform of positive theory. It is only because they found themselves disturbed in their peaceful and fruitful labors by the attacks of the Historical school, that they, like the farmer on the frontier who holds the plow with one hand and the sword with the other, have been constrained, almost against their will, to spend part of their time and strength in defensive polemics and in the solution of the problems of method forced upon them.

Features of Austrian Theory of Value—Final Utility

What, now, are the peculiar features which the Austrian school presents in the domain of positive theory?

Their researchers take their direction from the theory of value, the cornerstone being the well-known theory of final utility. This theory can be condensed into three unusually simple propositions. (1) The value of goods is measured by the importance of the want whose satisfaction is dependent upon the possession of the goods. (2) Which satisfaction is the dependent one can be determined very simply and infallibly by considering which want would be unsatisfied if the goods whose value is to be determined were not in possession. (3) And again, it is evident that the dependent satisfaction is not that satisfaction for the purpose of which the goods are actually used, but it is the least important of all the satisfactions which the total possessions of the individual can procure. Why? Because, according to very simple and unquestionably established prudential considerations of practical life, we are always careful to shift to the least sensitive point an injury to well-being which comes through loss of property. If we lose property

Böhm-Bawerk, "Grundzüge der Theorie des wirtschaftlichen Güterwerts," in Conrad's *Jahrbuch*, N.F., Vol. XIII, 1886, pp. 480ff. [Republished by London School of Economics and Political Science, 1932 (Reprint No. 11).] Review of Brentano's "Klassische Nationalökonomie in the *Göttinger Gelehrten Anzeigen*, 1–6, 1889. Review of Schmoller's "Literaturgeschichte" in Conrad's *Jahrbuch*, N.F., Vol. XX, 1890; translation "The Historical vs. the Deductive Method in Political Economy" in *Annals* of the American Academy, Vol. 1, No. 2, October, 1890.

that has been devoted to the satisfaction of a more important want, we do not sacrifice the satisfaction of this want, but simply withdraw other property which had been devoted to a less important satisfaction and put it in place of that which was lost. The loss thus falls upon the lesser utility, or—since we naturally give up the least important of all our satisfactions—upon the "final utility." Suppose a peasant has three sacks of corn: the first, *a*, for his support; the second, *b*, for seed; the third, *c*, for fattening poultry. Suppose sack *a* be destroyed by fire. Will the peasant on that account starve? Certainly not. Or will he leave his field unsown? Certainly not. He will simply shift the loss to the least sensitive point. He will bake his bread from sack *c*, and consequently fatten no poultry. What is, therefore, really dependent upon the burning or not burning of sack *a* is only the use of the least important unit which may be substituted for it, or, as we call it, the final utility.

As is well known, the fundamental principle of this theory of the Austrian school is shared by certain other economists. A German economist, Gossen, had enunciated it in a book of his which appeared in 1854, but at that time it attracted not the slightest attention.[3] Somewhat later the same principle was almost simultaneously discovered in three different countries, by three economists who knew nothing of one another and nothing of Gossen—by the Englishman W. S. Jevons,[4] by C. Menger, the founder of the Austrian school,[5] and by the Swiss, L. Walras.[6] Professor J. B. Clark, too, an American investigator, came very near the same idea.[7] But the direction in which I believe the Austrians have outstripped their rivals, is the use they have made of the fundamental idea in the subsequent construction of economic theory. The idea of final utility is to the expert the "Open sesame," as it were, by which he unlocks the most complicated phenomena of economic life and solves the hardest problems of the science. In this art of explication lies, as it seems to me, the peculiar strength and the characteristic significance of the Austrian school.

The Vital Point: Final Utility Rests on Substitution of Goods

And here everything turns upon one point: we need only take the trouble to discern the universal validity of the law of final utility

---

[3] *Entwicklung der Gesetze des menschlichen Verkehrs.*

[4] *Theory of Political Economy*, 1871, 2nd edition, 1879.

[5] *Grundsätze der Volkswirtschaftslehre*, 1871. [English translation: *Principles of Economics*, The Free Press, Glencoe, Ill., 1950; Grove City, Pa.: Libertarian Press, 1994.]

[6] *Eléments d'économie politique pure*, 1874. [English translation: *Elements of Pure Economics* (Homewood, Ill.: Irwin, 1954.]

[7] "Philosophy of Value," in the *New Englander*, July 1881. Professor Clark was not then familiar, as he tells me, with the works of Jevons and Menger.

throughout the manifold complications in which it is involved in the highly developed and varied economy of modern nations. This will cost us at the outset some trouble, but the effort will be well rewarded. For in the process we shall come upon all the important theoretical questions in their order and, what is the chief point, we shall approach them from the side from which they appear in their most natural form and from which we can most easily find a solution for them. I will attempt to make this plain for a few of the most important cases, at least so far as it is possible to do so without entering into details of theory.

The law of final utility rests, as we have seen, upon a peculiar substitution of goods, due to sound prudential considerations. Those goods which can most easily be dispensed with must always stand ready to fill the breach which may at any time be made at a more important point. In the case of our peasant with the sacks of corn, the cause and the consequence of the substitution are very easy to understand. But in highly developed economic relations, important complications take place, since the substitution of goods will extend in various directions beyond the supply of goods of the same species.

The First Complication, Arising from Exchange

The first complication is that due to exchange. If the only winter coat I possess be stolen, I shall certainly not go shivering and endanger my health, but I shall simply buy another winter coat with twenty dollars which I should otherwise have spent for something else. Of course, then, I can buy only twenty dollars' worth less of other goods, and, of course, I shall make the retrenchment in goods which I think I can most easily dispense with; *i.e.*, whose utility, as in the foregoing example, is the least; in a word, I shall dispense with the final utility. Satisfactions, therefore, which are dependent upon whether or not I lose my winter coat are the satisfactions that are most easily dispensed with, the satisfactions which, in the given condition of my property and income I could have procured with twenty dollars more; and it is upon those other satisfactions, which may be very different in nature, that, through the workings of substitution by exchange, the loss, and with it the final utility dependent on it, is shifted.[8]

---

[8] Böhm-Bawerk, *Grundzüge*, pp. 38 and 49 [also *Capital and Interest*. II, *Positive Theory of Capital*, pp. 151f.; *Wieser, Der natürliche Wert*, 1889, pp. 46ff. [English translation: *Natural Value*, New York: Kelley and Millman, Inc., 1956, pp. 47 ff.]

Escaping the "Circulus Vitiosus" of the Expression, Supply and Demand, as Explanation for Price

If we carefully follow out this complication we shall come upon one of the most important of theoretical problems: namely, upon the relation between the market price of given goods, and the subjective estimate which individuals set upon those goods according to their very various wants and inclinations on the one hand, and their property and income on the other. I will merely remark in passing that the complete solution of this problem requires very subtle investigation, which was first undertaken by the Austrian economists, and I will proceed to show the results which they have obtained. According to their conclusions, the price or "objective value" of goods is a sort of resultant of the different subjective estimates of the goods which the buyers and sellers make in accordance with the law of final utility; and indeed, the price coincides very nearly with the estimate of the "last buyer." It is well known that Jevons and Walras arrived at a similar law of price. Their statement, however, has considerable deficiencies which were first supplied by the Austrians. It was the latter who first found the right way of escape from the *circulus vitiosus* in which the older theory of price, as dependent upon supply and demand, was involved. Since it was undeniable that, on the one hand, the price which can be asked in the market is influenced by the estimate which the buyer sets upon the goods, but, on the other hand, it is just as undeniable that in many cases the buyer's estimate is influenced by the state of the market (as, for instance, the final utility of my winter coat is materially less when I can replace it in the market for *ten* dollars than when it costs me twenty dollars); the theorists who found a more exact psychological explanation necessary for the law of supply and demand in general[9] have usually allowed themselves to be beguiled into reasoning in a circle. They more or less openly explained the price by the estimate of the individual and, vice versa, the estimate of the individual by the price. Of course, such a solution is not one upon which a science that wishes to deserve the name of a science can rest. An attempt to get to the bottom of the matter was first made by the Austrian economists by means of the subtle investigation of which I have spoken above.[10]

---

[9] As, for example, in Germany, the highest authority on the theory of price, Hermann; cf. Böhm-Bawerk, *Grundzüge*, pp. 516, 527.

[10] Austrian literature on the subject of price: Menger, *Grundsätze der Volkswirtschaftslehre*, pp. 142ff. [*Principles*, 1950, pp. 164ff.]; Böhm-Bawerk, "Grundzüge der Theorie des wirtschaftlichen Güterwerts," Part II, Conrad's *Jahrbuch*, N.F., Vol. XIII, pp. 477ff., and on the point touched upon in the text, especially p. 516; Wieser, *Der natürliche Wert*, pp. 37ff.

The Second Complication, Arising from "Production"

A second interesting and difficult complication of the substitution of goods is due to *production:* namely, given a sufficient time, the goods whose substitution is under consideration could be replaced by production. As in the former case the goods were replaced by the use of money, so in this case they can be replaced directly by the conversion of materials of production. But, of course, there will be less of these materials of production left for other purposes and, just as surely as before, the necessary diminution of production will be shifted to that class of goods which can be most easily dispensed with, that which is considered least valuable.

Take Wieser's example:[11] If a nation finds weapons necessary to the defense of its honor or its existence, it will produce them from the same iron which would otherwise have been used for other necessary but more or less dispensable utensils. What, therefore, happens to the people through the necessity of procuring weapons is that they can have only somewhat less of the most dispensable utensils which they would have made of the iron; in other words, the loss falls upon the least utility, or the final utility, which could have been derived from the materials of production necessary to the manufacture of the weapons.

How the Foregoing Leads to the Determination of Value of Goods Producible at Will

From this point, again, the way leads to one of the most important theoretical principles, which under a certain form has long been familiar. This principle is that the value of those goods which can be reproduced at will without hindrance shows a tendency to coincide with the cost of production. This principle comes to light as a special case of the law of final utility occurring under given actual conditions. The "cost of production" is nothing else than the sum of all the materials of production by means of which the goods or a substitute for the same can be reproduced. Since then, as pointed out in the foregoing, the value of the goods is determined by the final utility of their substitute, it follows that so far as that substitution can be made *ad libitum,* the value of the

---

[*Natural Value,* 1956, pp. 39ff.]; Sax, *Grundlegung der theoretischen Staatswirtschaft,* 1887, pp. 276ff.; Zuckerkandl, *Zur Theorie des Preises,* 1889. I will not lose this opportunity to refer to the excellent account given by Dr. James Bonar some years ago of the Austrian economists and their view of value in the *Quarterly Journal of Economics,* October 1888 [reprinted in this volume, ed.].

[11] *Der natürliche Wert,* p. 170 [*Natural Value,* 1956].

product may coincide with the final utility and value of the materials of production or, as is usually said, with the cost of production.

"Cost" Is Not the Regulator of Value, But the Value of the Completed Product Determines the Value of Factors of Production Which Are Used

As to the final cause of this coincidence the Austrians have a theory quite different from the older one. The older theory explained the relation between cost and value to be such that cost was cause, indeed the final cause, while the value of the product was the effect. It supposed the scientific problem of explaining the value of goods to be satisfactorily solved when it had appealed to cost as the "ultimate regulator of value." The Austrians, on the contrary, believe that herein only half, and by far the easier half, of the explanation is to be found. The cost is identical with the value of the materials of production necessary to the manufacture of the goods. Cost rises when and because the materials of production (fuel, machinery, rent, labor) rise; it falls when and because the value of the materials declines. Hence, it is evident that the value of materials of production must first be explained. And the interesting point is that when the explanation is carefully carried out it leads us to see that the value of the completed product is the cause. For without doubt we place a high estimate upon materials of production only when and because they are capable of furnishing valuable products. The relation of cause and effect is, therefore, exactly the reverse of what the older theory stated. The older theory explained the value of the product as the effect, and the cost—that is, the value of the materials of production—as the cause, and thought no further explanation necessary. The Austrian economists found: (1) that, first of all, the value of the materials of production needs to be explained; and (2) that after this explanation is made, and after the net of complicated relations is untangled, the value of the materials of production is seen in the end to be the effect, and the value of the product the cause.

The Correct Principle Has Long Been Recognized in Specific Cases, But the General Principle Has Not Been Appreciated

I know very well that this thesis will seem strange to many readers at the first glance. I cannot here attempt to demonstrate it or even to guard it against certain misapprehensions to which it is liable. I will call attention to only one circumstance. In the case of certain materials of production, whose true causal connection was for special reasons easy to see, the old theory recognized the principle; for instance, in regard to the value of the use of land, which is expressed in rent, Adam Smith observed that the price of the products of the soil is not high or low because rent is high or low, but vice versa; rent is high or low according as the price of the product is high or low. Or again, no one supposes that copper is dear because the stock of the mining companies is high, but obviously the value of the mines and the stock is high when and because copper is dear. Now just as well might the water of one river flow up hill while that of the river beside it flows down as that in the case of different sorts of materials of production the causal connections should run in opposite directions. The law is one and the same for all materials of production. The difference is only that in case of certain materials the true relation of cause and effect is very easy to see, while in others, owing to manifold obscuring complications, it is very hard to see. The establishment of the law for those cases also, when deceptive appearances had led to the opposite explanation, is one of the most important contributions of the Austrian school.

Perhaps it is the most important of all. Every political economist knows what a vast part cost of production plays in the theory of political economy—in the theory of production no less than in that of value and price, and in this no less than in that of distribution, rent, wages, profit on capital, international trade, etc. It is safe to say that there is not one important phenomenon of economic life for the explanation of which we are not compelled either directly or indirectly to appeal to cost of production. And here rises the question which having once been thrown into the world is no more to be put out of it: What place does this much-appealed-to cost properly hold in the system of phenomena and their explanation? Does it play the part of a center about which as a fixed and absolute middle point all the other phenomena of value turn? Or is cost, the value of materials of production, in spite of all contradictory appearances, the variable part, determined by the value of the product?

Vacillation Is not Justified; Either Costs Regulate Value, or Value Regulates Cost

That is a question as fundamental for political economy as the question between the Ptolemaic and Copernican systems was for astronomy. The sun and earth turn, as every child knows, but one cannot be much of an astronomer today without knowing whether the earth turns about the sun or the sun about the earth. Between the value of the product and the value of the materials of production there exists a no less obvious and indubitable relation. But whoever wishes to understand this relation and the countless phenomena that depend upon it must know whether the value of the materials of production is derived from the value of the product or the reverse. From the first instant when this alternative comes into view in discussion everyone who wishes to be an economist must have an opinion, and a definite opinion. An eclectic vacillation, such as up to this time has been almost universal, will not do; in a scientific system we cannot have the earth turning about the sun and the sun turning about the earth alternately. Therefore, whoever today wishes to contend that the cost of production is "the ultimate regulator of value" may continue to do so; but he will not find his task so easy as it has been heretofore. We shall justly expect him to attempt to explain to the bottom, without deficiency or contradiction, in accordance with his principle, the phenomenon of value, and especially the value of materials of production. Probably, if he takes his task seriously, he will come upon difficulties. If he does not find them himself he must at least take account of those which others have met in the same path, by which they have finally been compelled to attempt the explanation of phenomena of value according to the opposite principle. At any rate, this part of economic theory will in the future be treated with a considerably greater degree of care and scientific profundity than has before now been customary, unless our science wishes to deserve the reproach which has both in former and later days been so often cast upon it; that economics is more a babbling over economic matters than a real, earnest science.[12]

The Problem of the Valuation of Complementary Goods

The question of the relation of cost to value is properly only a concrete form of a much more general question—the question of the regular relations between the values of such goods as in causal interdependence contribute to one and the same utility for our well-being. The utility furnished by a quantity of materials from which a coat can be produced is apparently identical with the utility which the completed coat will furnish. It is thus obvious that goods or groups of goods which derive their importance to our welfare through the medium of one and the same utility must also stand in some fixed, regular relation to one

---

[12] Austrian literature on the relation of cost and value: Menger, *Grundsätze*, pp. 123ff. [*Principles*, 1950, pp. 149ff.]; Wieser, *Über den Ursprung und die Hauptgesetze des wirtschaftlichen Wertes*, 1884, pp. 139ff.; *Der natürliche Wert*, pp. 164ff. [*Natural Value*, 1965, pp. 164ff]; Böhm-Bawerk, *Grundzüge*, pp. 61ff., 534ff.; *Positive Theorie des Kapitals*, 1889, pp. 189ff. [*Positive Theory*, 1959, pp. 121–256.]

another in respect to their value. The question of this regular relation was first put into clear and comprehensive form by the Austrian economists; it had previously been treated only in a very unsatisfactory manner under the head of "cost of production." There is, however, a corollary to this general and important proposition which is not less important and interesting, but which has hitherto never received the modest degree of attention in economic theory which has been bestowed upon the problem of cost. Very commonly several goods combine simultaneously to the production of one common utility; for example, paper, pen, and ink serve together for writing; needle and thread for sewing; farming utensils, seed, land and labor for the production of grain. Menger has called goods that stand in such relation to one another "complementary goods." Here rises the question, as natural as it is difficult: How much of the common utility is in such cases to be attributed to each of the cooperative complementary factors? And what law determines the proportionate value and price of each?

The fate of this problem hitherto has been very remarkable. The older theory did not rank it as a general problem at all, but was nevertheless compelled to decide a series of concrete cases which depended implicitly upon that problem. The question of the distribution of goods especially gave occasion for such decisions. Since several factors of production—soil, capital, hired labor, and labor of the employer himself—cooperate in the production of a common product, the question as to what share of value shall be assigned to each of the factors in compensation for its assistance is obviously a special case of the general problem.

The Old Bad Habit of Circular Reasoning on the Value of Complementary Goods

Now, how were these concrete cases decided? Each one was decided by itself without regard to others and hence, eventually, they formed a circle. The process was as follows: If rent was to be explained, it was decided that to the soil belonged the remainder of the product after the payment of cost of production, under which term was included the compensation of all the other factors—capital, labor, and profit of manager. Here the function of all the other factors was regarded as fixed or known and the soil was put off with a remainder varying according to the quantity of the product. If then it was necessary in another chapter to determine the profits of the entrepreneur, it was decided again that to him should be given the overplus left after all the other factors were compensated. In this case the share of the soil, the rent, was reckoned along with labor, capital, etc., as fixed, and the entrepreneur's profit was treated as the variable, rising and falling with the quantity of the product. In just the same manner the share of capital was treated in a third chapter. The capitalist, says Ricardo, receives what is left from the product after the payment of wages. And as if to satirize all these classical dogmas, last of all, Mr. F. A. Walker has completed the circle by stating that the laborer receives what is left over from all the other factors.

The Error of Attempting to Evade the General Problem

It is easy to see that these statements lead in a circle, and to see, also, why they so lead. The reasoners have simply neglected to state the problem in a general form. They had several unknown quantities to determine, and instead of taking the bull by the horns and straightway inquiring about the general principle, according to which a common economic result should be divided into its component factors, they tried to avoid the fundamental question—that of the general principle. They divided up the investigation, and in this partial investigation allowed themselves each time to treat as unknown that one of the unknown quantities which formed the special object of the investigation, but to treat the others, for the time being, as if known. They thus shut their eyes to the fact that a few pages earlier or later they had reversed the operation and had treated the supposed known quantity as unknown, the unknown as known.

After the Classical school came the Historical. As often happens, they took the attitude of skeptical superiority and declared altogether insoluble the problem which they were unable to solve. They thought it to be in general impossible to say, for example, what per cent of the value of a statue is due to the sculptor and what per cent to the marble.

Now if the problem be but rightly put, that is if we wish to separate the economic and not the physical shares, the problem becomes soluble. It is actually solved in practice in all rational enterprises by every agriculturalist or manufacturer and theory has nothing to do but rightly and carefully to hold up the mirror to practice in order in turn to find the theoretical solution. To this end the theory of final utility helps in the simplest way. It is the old song again. Only observe correctly what the final utility of each complementary factor is, or what utility the presence or absence of the complementary factor would add or subtract, and the calm pursuit of such inquiry will of itself bring to light the solution of the supposed insoluble problem. The Austrians made the first earnest attempt in this direction. Menger and the author of this paper have treated the question under the heading, *Theorie der komplementären Güter* (Theory of Complementary Goods). Wieser has treated the same subject under the title, *Theorie der Zurechnung* (Theory of Imputation). The latter, especially, has in an admirable manner shown how the problem should be put, and that it *can* be solved; Menger has, in the happiest manner, as it seems to me, pointed out the method of solution.[13]

I have called the law of complementary goods the counterpart of the law of cost. As the former disentangles the relations of value which result from temporal and causal *juxtaposition* from the simultaneous cooperation of several factors toward one common utility so the law of cost explains the relations of value, which result from temporal and causal *sequence,* from the causal interdependence of successive factors. "By means of the former the meshes of the complicated network represented by the mutual value relations of the cooperating factors are disentangled, so to speak, in their length and breadth; by the latter in their depth; but both processes occur within the all-embracing law of final utility, of which both laws are only special applications to special problems.[14]

Austrian Contributions to the Theories of Distribution, Capital, Wages, Profits and Rent

Thus prepared, the Austrian economists finally proceed to the problems of distribution. These resolve themselves into a series of special applications of the general theoretical laws, the knowledge of which was obtained by a tedious, but scarcely unfruitful, work of preparation. Land, labor, and capital are complementary factors of production. Their price, or what is the same thing, rate of rent, wages, and interest, results simply from a combination of the laws which govern the value of the materials of production on the one hand with the laws of complementary goods on the other hand. The particular views of the Austrians on these subjects I will here omit. I could not, if I would, give in this paper any proper statement of their conclusions, still less a demonstration of them; I must content myself with giving a passing view of the matters with which they are busied and, where it is possible, of the spirit in which they work. I only briefly remark, therefore,

---

[13] Menger, *Grundsätze,* pp. 138ff. [*Principles,* 1950, 162ff.]; Böhm-Bawerk, *Grundzüge,* Part I, pp. 56ff.; *Capital and Interest,* Vol. II: *Positive Theorie,* pp. 178ff. [*Positive Theory,* 1958, pp. 161–168]; Wieser, *Der Natürliche Wert,* pp. 67ff. [*Natural Value,* 1956, pp. 67ff].

[14] Böhm-Bawerk, *Capital and Interest,* Vol. II.: *Positive Theorie,* p. 201 [*Positive Theory,* 1959, pp. 121- 256, especially pp. 151–156, 161–168, 177, 248–256].

that they have set forth a new and comprehensive theory of capital[15] into which they have woven a new theory of wages,[16] besides repeatedly working out the problems of the entrepreneur's profits[17] and of rent.[18] In the light of the theory of final utility, the last-named problem in particular finds an easy and simple solution which confirms Ricardo's theory in its actual results and corroborates its reasoning in many details.

Of course, all the possible applications of the law of final utility have by no means been made. I may mention in passing that certain Austrian economists have attempted a broad application of the law in the field of finance;[19] others to certain difficult and interesting questions of jurisprudence.[20]

The Hitherto-Neglected Doctrine of Economic Goods

Finally, in connection with the foregoing efforts, much trouble has been taken to improve the implements, so to speak, with which the science has to work, to clear up the most important fundamental conceptions. And, as often happens, the Austrian economists find most to improve and correct in a department which has heretofore passed as so plain and simple that the literature of several nations—the English, for example—has scarcely a word to say about it. I refer to the doctrine of economic goods. Menger has put a logical implement into the hands of science in his concept, as simple as it is suggestive, of the orders of goods (*Güterordnungen*),[21] a concept which will be useful in all future investigation. The writer of this paper has especially endeavored to

---

[15] Böhm-Bawerk, *Kapital und Kapitalzins: I, Geschichte und Kritik der Kapitalzinstheorien*, 1884; II, *Positive Theorie des Kapitales*, 1889 [*Capital and Interest*, 1959, Libertarian Press, South Holland, Ill.: I, *History and Critique of Interest Theories*; II, *Positive Theory of Capital*; III, *Further Essays on Capital and Interest*]; differing from the older teaching of Menger's *Grundsätze*, pp. 143ff. [*Principles*, 1950, pp. 165ff.]

[16] Böhm-Bawerk, *Positive Theorie, passim* and pp. 450–452 [*Capital and Interest*, II: *Positive Theory*, 1959, pp. 308–312.]

[17] Mataja, *Der Unternehmergewinn*, 1884; Gross, *Die Lehre vom Unternehmergewinn*, 1884.

[18] Menger, *Grundsätze*, pp. 133ff. [*Principles*, 1950, pp. 157ff.]; Wieser, *Der natürliche Wert*, pp. 112ff. [*Natural Value*, 1956]; Böhm-Bawerk, *Positive Theorie*, pp. 380ff. [*Capital and Interest*, Vol. II: *Positive Theory*, 1959, pp. 334–337].

[19] Robert Meyer, *Die Prinzipien der gerechten Besteuerung*, 1884; Sax, *Grundlegung*, 1887; Wieser, *Der natürliche Wert*, pp. 209ff. [*Natural Value*, 1956].

[20] Mataja, *Das Recht des Schadenersatzes*, 1888; Seidler, "Die Geldstrafe vom volkswirtschaftlichen und sozialpolitischen Gesichtspunkt," Conrad's *Jahrbuch*, N. F. Vol. XX, 1890.

[21] Menger, *Grundsätze*, pp. 8ff. [*Principles*, 1950 pp. 55ff.].

analyze a concept which appears to be the simplest of all, but which is most obscure and most misused: the concept of the use of goods (*Gebrauch der Güter*).[22]

Increasing Attention to Practical Problems

Questions of practical political economy, on the contrary, have only just begun to be made the subjects of literary work by the Austrian economists.[23] This, however, by no means implies that they have no faculty for the practical needs of economic life, and still less, that they do not wish to connect their abstract theory with practice. The contrary is true. But we must build the house before we can set it in order, and so long as we have our hands full with simply raising the framework of our theory, there is little obligation to devote to numerous questions of practical detail that amount of time-absorbing care which their literary elaboration would require. We have our opinions upon them, we teach them from our chairs, but our literary activities have thus far been bestowed almost exclusively upon theoretical problems, for these are not only the fundamental ones, but are those whose long-continued neglect by the other side, the Historical school, must be repaired.

Purpose of the Austrians; Renaissance of Economic Theory; Character of that Renaissance

What, now, is the short meaning of this long story? What is the significance to the science as a whole of the advent of a set of men who teach this and that in regard to goods, value, cost, capital, and a dozen other subjects? Has it any significance at all? In answering this question I feel the embarrassment of belonging to the group of men whose activity is under discussion. I must, therefore, confine myself to the statement of what the Austrian economists as a body are trying to effect; others may judge whether or not they are successful.

What they are striving for is a sort of *renaissance* of economic theory. The old Classical theory, admirable as it was for its time, had the character of a collection of fragmentary acquisitions which had been

---

[22] Böhm-Bawerk, *Rechte und Verhältnisse vom Standpunkt der volkswirtschaftlichen Güterlehre*, 1881, pp. 57ff. [English translation: *Whether Legal Rights and Relationships Are Economic Goods*, pp. 70ff. included in *Shorter Classics of Eugen von Böhm-Bawerk* (South Holland, Ill.: Libertarian Press, 1962); *Positive Theorie*, pp. 361ff. [*Positive Theory*, 1959, pp. 325ff.].

[23] By Sax, for example, *Die Verkehrsmittel in Volks- und Staatswirtschaft*, 1878–79; Philippovich, *Die Bank von England*, 1885; *Der badische Staatshaushalt*, 1889.

brought into orderly relations neither with one another nor with the fundamental principles of human science. Our knowledge is only patchwork at best, and must always remain so. But of the Classical theory this characterization was particularly and emphatically true. With the insight of genius it had discovered a mass of regularities in the whirlpool of economic phenomena and with no less genius, though hindered by the difficulties that beset beginnings, it commenced the interpretation of these regularities. It usually succeeded, also, in following the thread of explanation to a greater or lesser distance from the surface toward the depths. But beyond a certain depth it always, without exception, lost the clue. To be sure, the Classical economists well knew to what point all their explanations must be traced—to the care of mankind for its own well-being which, undisturbed by the incursion of altruistic motives, is the ultimate motive-force of all economic action. But owing to a certain circumstance the middle term of the explanation—by means of which the actual conduct of men, in the establishment of prices of goods, wages, rent, etc., ought to have been joined to the fundamental motive of regard for utility—was always wrong. That circumstance was the following: A Crusoe has to do only with goods; in modern economic life we have to do with goods and with human beings from whom we obtain the goods we use—by means of exchange, cooperation, and the like. The economy of a Crusoe is explained when we succeed in showing what relation exists between our well-being and material commodities, and what attitude the care for our well-being requires us to take toward such material commodities. To explain the modern economic order there is apparently need of two processes: (1) just as in Crusoe's economy, we must understand the relation of our interests to external goods; and (2) we must seek to understand the laws, according to which we pursue our interests when they are entangled with the interests of others.

Two Distinct Problems: Relations of Men to Things; Relations of Men to Each Other

No one has ever been deluded into thinking that this second process is not difficult and involved—not even the Classical economists. But, on the other hand, they fatally underrated the difficulties of the first process. They believed that as regards the relation of men to external goods, there was nothing at all to be explained or, speaking more exactly, determined. Men need goods to supply their wants; men desire them and assign to them in respect of their utility a value in use. That is all the Classical economists knew or taught in regard to the relation of men to goods. While value in exchange was discussed and explained in extensive chapters, from the time of Adam Smith to that of Mr. MacVane, value in use was commonly dismissed in two lines, and often with the added statement that value in use had nothing to do with value in exchange.

Past Underestimation of Problems of Relations of Men to Things; the Yawning Defect of Classical Economics

It is a fact, however, that the relation of men to goods is by no means so simple and uniform. The modern theory of final utility in its application to cost of production, complementary goods, etc., shows that the relation between our well-being and goods is capable of countless degrees, and all these degrees exert a force in our efforts to obtain goods by exchange with others. Here yawns the great and fatal chasm in the Classical theory; it attempts to show how we pursue our interests in relation to goods in opposition to other men without thoroughly understanding the interest itself. Naturally the attempts at explanation are incoherent. The two processes of explanation must fit together like the two cogwheels of a machine. But as the Classical economists had no idea what the shape and cogging of the first wheel should be, of course they could not give to the second wheel a proper constitution. Thus, beyond a certain depth, all their explanations degenerate into a few general commonplaces, and these are fallacious in their generalization.

This is the point at which the renaissance of theory must begin and, thanks to the efforts of Jevons and his followers as well as to the Austrian school, it has already begun. In that most general and elementary part of economic theory through which every complicated economic explanation must eventually lead, we must give up *dilettanti* phrases for real scientific inquiry. We must not weary of studying the microcosm if we wish rightly to understand the macrocosm of a developed economic order. This is the turning-point which is reached at one time or another in all sciences. We universally begin by taking account of the great and striking phenomena, passing unobservant over the world of little every-day phenomena. But there always comes a time when we discover with astonishment that the complications and riddles of the macrocosm occur in still more remarkable manner in the smallest, apparently simplest elements—when we apprehend that we must seek the key to an understanding of the phenomena of great things in the study of the world of small things. The physicists began with the motions and laws of the great heavenly bodies; today they are studying nothing more busily than the theory of the molecule and the atom, and from no part of natural science do we expect more important developments for the eventual understanding of the whole than from the minutiae of chemistry. In the organic world the most highly developed and mightiest organisms once roused the greatest interest. Today that interest is given to the simplest microorganisms. We study the structure of cells and of amoebae, and look everywhere for bacilli. I am convinced that it will not be otherwise in economic theory. The significance of the theory of final utility does not lie in the fact that it is a more correct theory of value than a dozen other older theories. Rather, its significance lies in the fact that it marks the approach of that characteristic crisis in the science of economic phenomena; it shows for once that in an apparently simple thing, the relation of man to external goods, there is room for endless complications, that underneath these complications lie fixed laws, the discovery of which demands all the acumen of the investigator, but that in the discovery of those laws is accomplished the greater part of the investigation of the conduct of men in economic intercourse with one another. The candle lighted within sheds its light outside the house.

Discontent with the Necessity of Rebuilding the Science of Economics Is Not Apropos; We Must Build Better than the Pioneers in Economics

It may, of course, be to many who call themselves political economists a very inconvenient and unpleasant surprise to find that to the field which they have heretofore ploughed with intellectual toil, another new field is added—a field by no means small, whose tillage is particularly laborious. How convenient it has been heretofore to conclude an explanation of phenomena of price with reference to the shibboleth of "supply and demand" or "cost"! And now, on a sudden, these supposed pillars tremble, and we are forced to build the foundations far deeper, at the cost of great and tedious labor.

Whether inconvenient or not, there is no other course left us than to do the work which past generations have neglected. The Classical economists are excusable for having neglected it. In their time, when everything was yet new and undiscovered, investigation *per saltum* [at a single bound], scientific exploitation, so to speak, might bring rich results. But now it is otherwise. In the first place, we of later times, since we have not the merit of being pioneers of the science, should not lay claim to the privilege of pioneers: the requirements have become higher. If we do not wish to remain behind the other sciences, we too must bring into our science a strict order and discipline, which we are still far from having. Let us not be beguiled into vain self-satisfaction. Mistakes and omissions are, of course, to be expected at any time in every science, but our "systems" still swarm with the commonplace, superficial faults whose frequent occurrence is a sure sign of the primitive state of a science. That our expositions end in smoke before essentials are reached, that they evaporate in empty phrases as soon as they begin to be difficult, that the most important problems are not even stated, that we reason in the most undisguised circle, that not only within the same system, but even within the same chapter, contradictory theories of one and the same matter are upheld, that by a disorderly and ambiguous terminology we are led into the most palpable mistakes and misunderstandings—all these failings are of so frequent occurrence in our science that they almost seem to be characteristic of its style. I can easily understand how the representatives of other sciences, which have become amenable to strict discipline, look down with a sort of pity upon many a famous work of political economy, and deny to the latter the character of a true science.

The German Historical School Has Not Contributed Much to Solution of the Problem of Improving Economics

This state of affairs must and shall be changed. The Historical school, which for the last forty years has given the keynote to all Germany, has unfortunately done nothing at all to this end. On the contrary, in its blind terror of "abstract" reasoning and through the cheap skepticism with which at almost every important point in the system it declares the given problems "insoluble" and the struggles to discover scientific laws hopeless, it has done its utmost to discourage and obstruct the scanty efforts that have been directed toward the desired end. I do not ignore the fact that in another direction, in the provision of vast empirical stores, they have conferred great benefit, but future time will impartially show how much they have helped in this direction and how much they have harmed in the other with their one-sided zeal.

But what both the Classical and the Historical schools have neglected, the Austrian school is today trying to accomplish. Nor are they alone in the struggle. In England, since the days of Jevons, kindred efforts, to which the great thinker gave the impulse, have been carried forward by his worthy associates and followers. Incited partly by Jevons, partly by the Austrian school, a surprisingly great number of investigators, of all nations, have in recent times turned to the new ideas. The great Dutch literature is devoted almost entirely to them. In France, Denmark, and Sweden they have gained an entrance. In Italian and American literature they are almost daily propagated. And even in Germany, the stronghold of the Historical school against whose resistance the ground must be fought for almost inch by inch, the new tendency has taken a strong and influential position.

Can the tendency which possesses so great a power of attraction be nothing but error? Or does this new tendency spring in reality from a need of our science, a need which has long been repressed by one-sided methods, but which must eventually make itself felt—the need of real scientific depth?

Remarks on the Fundamental Problem of the Subjective Theory of Value[1]

by Ludwig von Mises

The following essay makes no claim to originality. It presents nothing that was not already contained at least implicitly in the writings of the founders of the modern theory and explicitly in the works of present-day theorists and in my own writings. Nevertheless, I believe that what I am about to present here must be said once again, and precisely in this form, in order to put an end to the serious misunderstandings that modern economic theory repeatedly encounters.

What needs to be especially emphasized is that, above all others, Menger and Böhm-Bawerk include propositions and concepts carried over from the objective theory of value and therefore utterly incompatible with the subjectivism of the modern school. The problem arises not so much from imperfections of theory, because there can be no doubt about the fundamental ideas of their system, as from stylistic faults in the presentation of it, which do not detract from the thought but only from the writings in which it was expounded. It was not difficult for those who came afterward to find the right way and to present the ideas of the masters in logically developed form. But it may be conceded that it is not easy for everyone to avoid error here. The great many who want to study the system, but who are not professional economists and turn only to the works of its masters, or who view subjectivist economics merely from the fractional standpoint of its opponents, cannot help being led astray.

I

The subjective theory of value traces the exchange ratios of the market back to the consumers' subjective valuations of economic goods. For catallactics the ultimate relevant cause of the exchange ratios of the market is the fact that the individual, in the act of exchange,

---

[1] First published in 1928, included in *Grundprobleme der Nationalökonomie* (1933). [English translation: *Epistemological Problems of Economics.* Translated from the German by George Reisman (Princeton, N.J.: D. Van Nostrand, 1960; New York: New York University Press, 1981)]. This chapter reprinted here by permission.

prefers a definite quantity of good A to a definite quantity of good B. The reasons he may have for acting exactly thus and not otherwise—for example, the reasons why someone buys bread, and not milk, at a given moment—are of absolutely no importance for the determination of a market price. What is alone decisive is that the parties on the market are prepared to pay or to accept this price for bread and that price for milk. Individuals as consumers value goods exactly so much and no more or less at a given moment because of the operation of the social and the natural forces that determine their lives. The investigation of these determining factors is the task of other sciences, not that of economics. Economics, the science of catallactics, does not concern itself with them and, from its standpoint, cannot concern itself with them. Psychology, physiology, cultural history, and many other disciplines may make it their business to investigate why men like to drink alcohol; for catallactics what is alone of importance is that a demand for alcoholic beverages exists in a definite volume and strength. One person may buy Kant's works out of a thirst for knowledge; another, for reasons of snobbery. For the market, the motivation of the buyers' actions is indifferent. All that counts is that they are prepared to spend a definite sum.

This and nothing else is the essential element of the economic theory of wants. Only the historical development of economics as a science can explain why the meaning of this theory could be so much misunderstood that many even wanted to assign it entirely to psychology and to separate it altogether from catallactics, and still others could see in it only a materialistic theory of value and utility. The great problem with which economics has been incessantly occupied since its founding in the eighteenth century is the establishment of a relationship between human well-being and the valuing of the objects of economic action by economizing individuals. The older theory did not recognize that economic action in a social order based on private property is never an action of the whole of mankind, but always the action of individuals, and that it generally does not aim at the disposal of the entire supply of a good of a given type, but merely at the utilization of a definite part. Hence arose the problem of the paradox of value, which the earlier theory was helpless to resolve. Accordingly, in the treatment of the problem of value and price determination it was shunted onto a wrong track, became entangled more and more in a morass of untenable theorems, and finally failed completely.

The great service that modern economics performed consists in resolving the paradox of value. This was effected by the realization that economic action is always divided only toward the utilization of definite quantities of a good. Böhm-Bawerk said:

If I have to buy a horse, it will not occur to me to form an opinion about how much a hundred horses, or how much all the horses in the world, would be worth to me, and then to adjust my bid accordingly; but I shall, of course, make a judgment of value about one horse. And in this way, by virtue of an inner compulsion, we always make exactly that value judgment which the concrete situation requires.[2]

Economic action is always in accord only with the importance that acting man attaches to the limited quantities among which he must directly choose. It does not refer to the importance that the total supply at his disposal has for him nor to the altogether impractical judgment of the social philosopher concerning the importance for humanity of the total supply that men can obtain. The recognition of this fact is the essence of the modern theory. It is independent of all psychological and ethical considerations. However, it was advanced at the same time as the law of the satiation of wants and of the decrease in the marginal utility of the unit in an increasing supply. All attention was turned toward this law, and it was mistakenly regarded as the chief and basic law of the new theory. Indeed, the latter was more often called the theory of diminishing marginal utility than the doctrine of the subjectivist school, which would have been more suitable and would have avoided misunderstandings.

II

The fact that modern economics starts from acting man's subjective valuations and the action that is governed by these valuations, and not from any kind of objectively "correct" scale of values, is so familiar to everyone who is even slightly conversant with modern catallactics or who has thought only very little about the meaning of the terms "supply" and "demand" that it would be out of place to waste any more words on it. That it is frequently attacked by authors whose stand is opposed to that of subjective economics—for example, recently by Diehl[3]—is the result of such crass misunderstanding of the entire the-

---

[2] *Cf.* Böhm-Bawerk, "Grunzüge der Theorie des wirtschaftlichen Güterwerts," *Jahrbücher für Nationalökonomie und Statistik*, New Series, XIII, 16; also *Kapital und Kapitalzins* (3rd ed.: Innsbruck, 1909), Part II, p. 228 [English translation, *Capital and Interest*, II, Libertarian Press, 1959, p. 131]. Editor's Note: For complete citation see footnote 2 of Böhm-Bawerk's *Annals* article (above).

[3] *Cf.* Diehl, *Theoretische Nationalökonomie* (Jena, 1916), I, 287; (Jena, 1927), III, 82–87. Against this, cf. Mises' essays in *Archiv für Geschichte des Sozialismus*, X, 93 ff.

ory that it can be passed over without further discussion. Modern economics cannot be more clearly characterized than by the phrase "subjective use value." The explanation that the new theory gives of the phenomena of the market does not have as its basis any "scale of wants which is constructed on rational principles,"[4] as Diehl maintains. The scale of wants or of values, of which the theory speaks, is not "constructed." We infer it from the action of the individual or even—whether or not this is permissible can remain undecided here—from his statements about how he would act under certain assumed conditions.

Diehl considers it obviously absurd to draw on "fanciful wishes, desires, etc." for an explanation and thinks that in that case value would be determined by "the subjective whims of each individual" and thereby "the theory of marginal utility would lose all meaning."[5] Here he has indeed been misled by the oft-lamented ambiguity of the term "value," whose meaning for catallactics must not be confused with the "absolute" values of ethics. For no one will want to doubt that market prices, the formation of which we have to explain, really are influenced by "fanciful wishes" and caprices in exactly the same way as by motives that appear rational in Diehl's eyes. Let Diehl try some time to explain, without referring to "fanciful wishes and desires," the formation of the prices of goods that fluctuate in response to changes in fashion! Catallactics has the task of explaining the formation of the exchange ratios of economic goods that are actually observed in the market, and not those which would come about if all men were to act in a way that some critic regards as rational.

All this is so clear, as has been said, that no one will doubt it. It cannot be the task of this essay to belabor the obvious by attempting to prove it in detail. On the contrary, what we intend is something altogether different. We have already pointed out that Menger and Böhm-Bawerk made statements in various passages of their writings that are utterly incompatible with the basic principles they advanced. It should not be forgotten that the two masters, like all pioneers and trail blazers, had first assimilated the old concepts and ideas that had come down from earlier days and only later substituted more satisfactory concepts and ideas for them. It is humanly excusable, even if it is not objectively justifiable, that occasionally they were not consistent in the elaboration of their great fundamental ideas and that in details they clung to assertions stemming from the conceptual structure of the old, objective the-

---

[4] *Loc. cit.*, Vol. III, p. 85.
[5] *Ibid.*

ory of value. A critical consideration of this insufficiency of the work of the founders of the Austrian school is an absolute necessity, since they seem to present great difficulties to many readers who attempt to understand the theory. For this reason I wish to select a passage from the chief work of each.[6]

In the preface to the first edition of his *Principles of Economics,* Menger describes the "proper subject matter of our science," i.e., theoretical economics, as the investigation of the "conditions under which men display provisionary activity that aims at the satisfaction of their wants." He illustrates this in the following words:

> Whether and under what conditions a thing is useful to me; whether and under what conditions it is a good; whether and under what conditions it is an economic good; whether and under what conditions it has value to me, and how great the measure of this value is to me; whether and under what conditions an economic exchange of goods between two parties can take place; and the margins within which prices can be formed in such an exchange; and so on.[7]

This, according to Menger, is the subject matter of economics It should be noted how the subjectivity of the phenomena of value is repeatedly emphasized by means of the personal pronoun "me": "useful to me," "value to me," "measure of this value to me," etc.

Unfortunately, Menger did not adhere to this principle of subjectivity in his description of the qualities that make things goods in the economic sense. Although he cites Storch's beautiful definition (*l'arrêt que notre jugement porte sur l'utilité des choses. . . en fait des biens* [the attachment which our judgment brings to the utility of things—in their service as goods]), he declares that the presence of all four of the following prerequisites is necessary for a thing to become a good:

1. A human want.
2. Such properties of the thing as enable it to be placed in a causal relation with the satisfaction of this want.

---

[6] With regard to the problem of the measurement of value and of total value, not treated further here, I [Mises] have examined critically the works of a few of the older representatives of the modern theory of value in *The Theory of Money and Credit* (Yale University Press, 1953, pp. 38–47 [Liberty Fund, 1980, pp. 51–60]).

[7] Menger, *Grundsätze der Volkswirtschaftslehre* (Vienna, 1871), p. ix; (2nd ed., Vienna, 1923), p. xxi. English translation, *The Principles of Economics,* p. 48.

3. Knowledge of this causal relation on the part of a human being.

4. The ability to direct the employment of the thing in such a way that it actually can be used for the satisfaction of this want.[8]

The fourth prerequisite does not concern us here. There is nothing to criticize in the first requirement. As far as it is understood in this connection, it corresponds completely to the fundamental ideal of subjectivism, viz., that in the case of the individual he alone decides what is or is not a need. Of course, we can only conjecture that this was Menger's opinion when he wrote the first edition. It is to be noted that Menger cited Roscher's definition (everything that is acknowledged as useful for the satisfaction of a *real* human want) along with many definitions[9] of other predecessors, without going further into the matter.

However, in the posthumous second edition of his book, which appeared more than half a century later and which (apart from the section on money published long before in the *Handwörterbuch der Staatswissenschaften*) can in no way be called an improvement over the epoch-making first edition, Menger distinguishes between real and imaginary wants. The latter are those

> . . .which do not in fact originate from the nature of the person or from his position as a member of a social body, but are only the results of defective knowledge of the exigencies of his nature and of his position in human society.[10]

Menger adds the observation:

> The practical economic life of men is determined not by their wants, but by their momentary opinions about the exigencies of the preservation of their lives and well-being; indeed, often by their lusts and instincts. Rational theory and practical economics will have to enter into the investigation of real wants, i.e., wants which correspond to the objective state of affairs.[11]

To refute this notorious slip it suffices to quote some of Menger's own words a few lines before those just cited. There we read:

---

[8] *Cf.* Menger, *op. cit.* (1st ed.), p. 3; English translation, p. 52.

[9] *Ibid.*, p. 2n; English translation, pp. 287–288.

[10] *Ibid.*, 2nd ed., p. 4. (N.B. The 2nd, 1923, posthumous edition of Menger's book has not been translated.)

[11] *Ibid.*, p. 4 *et seq.*

The opinion that physical wants alone are the subject matter of
our science is erroneous. The conception of it as merely a theory of the physical well-being of man is untenable. If we
wished to limit ourselves exclusively to the consideration of
the physical wants of men, we should be able, as we shall see,
to explain the phenomena of human economic action only very
imperfectly and in part not at all.[12]

Here Menger has said all that needs to be said on this subject. The case
is exactly the same with regard to the distinction between real and
imaginary wants as it is in regard to the distinction between physical
and nonphysical wants.

It follows from the preceding quotations that the second and the
third prerequisites for a thing to become a good would have to read: the
opinion of the economizing individuals that the thing is capable of satisfying their wants. This makes it possible to speak of a category of
"imaginary" goods. The case of imaginary goods, Menger maintains, is
to be observed

. . . where things which in no way can be placed in a causal relation with the satisfaction of human wants are nonetheless
treated as goods. This happens when properties, and thus
effects, are attributed to things to which in reality they do not
belong or when human wants that in reality are not present are
falsely presumed to exist.[13]

To realize how pointless this dichotomy between real and imaginary
goods is, one need only consider the examples cited by Menger. Among
others, he designates as imaginary goods utensils used in idolatry, most
cosmetics, etc. Yet prices are demanded and offered for these things too,
and we have to explain these prices.

In the words of C. A. Verrijn Stuart, the basis of subjective use value
is described very differently, but completely in the spirit of the theories
that Menger elaborated in the latter sections of his basic work: A man's
valuation of goods is based on "his insight into their usefulness," in
which sense anything can be conceived as useful "that is the goal of any
human desire, whether justified or not. It is for this reason that such
goods can satisfy a human want."[14]

---

[12] *Ibid.*, p. 5.
[13] *Ibid.*, p. 4; 2nd ed., pp. 161 ff.
[14] C. A. Verrijn Stuart, *Die Grundlagen der Volkswirtschaft* (Jena, 1923), p. 94.

III

Böhm-Bawerk expresses the opinion that the treatment of the theory of price determination should be divided into two parts.

> The first part has the task of formulating the law of the fundamental phenomenon in all its purity; that is, to deduce all propositions following from the law that lead to the phenomena of prices on the hypothesis that for all persons interested in exchange the only impelling motive is the desire to attain a direct gain in the transaction. To the second part falls the task of combining the law of the fundamental phenomenon with modifications that result from factual conditions and the emergence of other motives. This will be the place to . . . demonstrate the influence that such commonly felt and typical "motives" as habit, custom, fairness, humanity, generosity, comfort or convenience, pride, race and nationality, hatred, etc. have in the determination of prices.[15]

In order to arrived at a correct judgment of this argument, one must note the difference that exists between classical and modern economics in the starting points of their investigations. Classical economics starts from the action of the businessman in that it places exchange value, and not use value, at the center of its treatment of the problem of price determination. Since it could not succeed in resolving the paradox of value, it had to forgo tracing the phenomenon of price determination further back and disclosing what lies behind the conduct of the businessman and governs it in every instance, viz., the conduct of the marginal consumers. Only a theory of utility, i.e., of subjective use value, can explain the action of the consumers. If such a theory cannot be formulated, any attempt at an explanation must be renounced. One certainly was not justified in leveling against the Classical theory the reproach that it starts from the assumption that all men are businessmen and act like members of a stock exchange. However, it is true that the Classical doctrine was not capable of comprehending the most fundamental element of economics—consumption and the direct satisfaction of a want.

Because the Classical economists were able to explain only the action of businessmen and were helpless in the face of everything that

---

[15] *Cf.* Böhm-Bawerk, *Kapital und Kapitalzins,* II, 354. English translation, *Capital and Interest,* II, p. 212.

went beyond it, their thinking was oriented toward bookkeeping, the supreme expression of the rationality of the businessman (but not that of the consumer). Whatever cannot be entered into the businessman's accounts they were unable to accommodate in their theory. This explains several of their ideas—for example, their position in regard to personal services. The performance of a service which caused no increase in value that could be expressed in the ledger of the businessman had to appear to them as unproductive. Only thus can it be explained why they regarded the attainment of the greatest monetary profit possible as the goal of economic action. Because of the difficulties occasioned by the paradox of value, they were unable to find a bridge from the realization, which they owed to utilitarianism that the goal of action is an increase of pleasure and a decrease of pain, to the theory of value and price. Therefore, they were unable to comprehend any change in well-being that cannot be valued in money in the account books of the businessman.

This fact necessarily led to a distinction between economic and noneconomic action. Whoever sees and grasps the opportunity to make the cheapest purchase (in money) has acted economically. But whoever has purchased at a higher price than he could have, either out of error, ignorance, incapacity, laziness, neglectfulness, or for political, nationalistic, or religious reasons has acted noneconomically. It is evident that this grading of action already contains an ethical coloration. A norm soon develops from the distinction between the two groups of motives: You should act economically; you should buy in the cheapest market and sell in the dearest market; in buying and selling you should know no other goal than the greatest monetary profit.

It has already been shown that the situation is altogether different for the subjective theory of value. There is little sense in distinguishing between economic and other motives in explaining the determination of prices if one starts with the action of the marginal consumer and not with that of the businessman.

This can be clearly illustrated by an example drawn from the conditions of a politically disputed territory, let us say Czechoslovakia. A German intends to join a chauvinistic, athletic-military organization and wants to acquire the necessary outfit and paraphernalia for it. If he could make this purchase more cheaply in a store run by a Czech, then we should have to say, if we make such a distinction among motives, that in buying at a slightly higher price in a store run by a German in order to give his business to a fellow national, he would be acting uneconomically. Yet it is clear that the whole purchase as such would have to be called uneconomic, since the procuring of the outfit itself is to serve a chauvinistic purpose just as much as helping a fellow national by not considering the possibility of making a cheaper purchase from a foreigner. But then many other expenditures would have to be called uneconomic, each according to the taste of whoever judges them: contributions for all kinds of cultural or political purposes, expenditures for churches, most educational expenses, etc. One can see how ridiculous such scholastic distinctions are. The maxims of the businessman cannot be applied to the action of the consumers, which, in the last analysis, governs all business.

On the other hand, it is possible for the subjective theory of value to comprehend from its standpoint also the action of the businessman (whether he is a manufacturer or only a merchant) precisely because it starts from the action of the consumers. Under the pressure of the market the businessman must always act in accordance with the wishes of the marginal consumers. For the same reason that he cannot, without suffering a loss, produce fabrics that do not suit the taste of the consumers, he cannot, without taking a loss, act on the basis of political considerations that are not acknowledged and accepted by his customers. Therefore, the businessman must purchase from the cheapest source, without any such considerations, if those whose patronage he seeks are not prepared, for political reasons, to compensate him for his increased expenses in paying higher prices to a fellow national. But if the consumers themselves—let us say in purchasing trademarked articles—are prepared to compensate him, he will conduct his business affairs accordingly.

If we take the other examples cited by Böhm-Bawerk and go through the whole series, we shall find the same thing in each case. Custom requires that in the evening a man of "good" society appear in evening clothes. If somewhere the prejudices of the circle in which he lives demand that the suit not come from the shop of a *radical* tailor, where it can be bought more cheaply, but that it be procured from the more expensive shop of a tailor with *conservative* leanings, and if our man acts in accordance with these views, he follows no other motive in doing so than that of getting a suit in general. In both instances, in agreeing to purchase evening clothes in the first place, and in procuring them from the tailor with conservative leanings, he acts in accordance with the views of his circle, which he acknowledges as authoritative for himself.

What is that "direct gain in the exchange" which Böhm-Bawerk speaks of? When, for humanitarian reasons, I do not buy pencils in the stationery store, but make my purchase from a war-wounded peddler who asks a higher price, I aim at two goals at the same time: that of obtaining pencils and that of assisting an invalid. If I did not think this second purpose worthy of the expense involved, I should buy in the store. With the more expensive purchase I satisfy two wants: that for pencils and that of helping a war veteran. When, for reasons of "comfort and convenience," I pay more in a nearby store rather than buy more cheaply in one further away, I satisfy my desire for "comfort and convenience," in the same way as by buying an easy chair or by using a taxi or by hiring a maid to keep my room in order. It cannot be denied that in all these instances I make a "direct gain in the exchange" in the sense intended by Böhm-Bawerk. Why, then, should the case be any different when I buy in a nearby store?

Böhm-Bawerk's distinction can be understood only when it is recognized as a tenet taken over from the older, objective system of Classical economics. It is not at all compatible with the system of subjective economics. But in saying this, we must emphasize that such a dichotomy had not the slightest influence on Böhm-Bawerk's theory of value and price determination and that the pages in which it is propounded could be removed from his book without changing anything significant in it. In the context of this work it represents nothing more than—as we believe we have shown—an unsuccessful defense against the objections that had been raised against the possibility of a theory of value and price determination.

Strigl expresses the matter more nearly in accordance with the subjective system than does Böhm-Bawerk. He points out that the scale of values "is fundamentally composed also of elements that popular usage treats as noneconomic in contrast to the economic principle." Therefore, the "maximum quantity of available goods cannot be opposed as 'economic,' to the 'uneconomic' goals of action." [16]

For the comprehension of economic phenomena it is quite permissible to distinguish "purely economic" action from other action which, if one wishes, may be called "noneconomic," or "uneconomic" in popular usage, provided it is understood that "purely economic" action is necessarily susceptible of calculation in terms of money. Indeed, both for the scientific study of phenomena and for the practical conduct of men, there may even be good reason to make this distinction and perhaps to say that under given conditions it is not advisable, from the "purely economic" point of view to manifest a certain conviction or that some course of action is "bad business," that is to say, it cannot involve a monetary gain, but only losses. If, nevertheless, one persists

---

[16] Strigl, *Die ökonomischen Kategorien und die Organisation der Wirtschaft* (Jena, 1923), p. 75 *et seq. Cf.* further *ibid.*, pp. 146ff.

in acting in that way, he has done so not for the sake of monetary gain, but for reasons of honor or loyalty or for the sake of other ethical values. But for the theory of value and price determination, catallactics, and theoretical economics, this dichotomy has no significance. For it is a matter of complete indifference for the exchange ratios of the market, the explanation of which is the task of these disciplines, whether the demand for domestic products arises because they cost less money than foreign goods (of the same quality, of course) or because nationalist ideology makes the purchase of domestic products even at a higher price seem right; just as, from the point of view of economic theory, the situation remains the same whether the demand for weapons comes from honorable men who want to enforce the law or from criminals who are planning monstrous crimes.

IV

The much talked about *homo oeconomicus* of the Classical theory is the personification of the principles of the businessman. The businessman wants to conduct every business with the highest possible profit: he wants to buy as cheaply as possible and sell as dearly as possible. By means of diligence and attention to business he strives to eliminate all sources of error so that the results of his action are not prejudiced by ignorance, neglectfulness, mistakes, and the like.

Therefore, the *homo oeconomicus* is not a fiction in Vaihinger's sense. Classical economics did not assert that the economizing individual, whether engaged in trade or as a consumer, acts as if the greatest monetary profit were the sole guiding principle of his conduct. The Classical scheme is not at all applicable to consumption or the consumer. It could in no way comprehend the act of consumption or the consumer's expenditure of money. The principle of buying on the cheapest market comes into question here only insofar as the choice is between several possibilities, otherwise equal, of purchasing goods; but it cannot be understood, from this point of view, why someone buys the better suit even though the cheaper one has the same "objective" usefulness, or why more is generally spent than is necessary for the minimum—taken in the strictest sense of the term—necessary for bare physical subsistence. It did not escape even the Classical economists that the economizing individual, as a party engaged in trade does not always and cannot always remain true to the principles governing the businessman; he is not omniscient; he can err; and, under certain conditions, he even prefers his comfort to a profit-making business.

On the contrary, it could be said that, with the scheme of the *homo oeconomicus,* Classical economics comprehended only one side of man—the economic, materialistic side. It observed him only as a man engaged in business, not as a consumer of economic goods. This would be a pertinent observation insofar as the Classical theory is inapplicable to the conduct of the consumers. On the other hand, it is not a pertinent observation insofar as it is understood as meaning that, according to Classical economic theory, a person engaged in business always acts in the manner described. What Classical economics asserts is only that in general he tends to act in this way, but that he does not always conduct himself, with or without such an intention, in conformity with this principle.

Yet neither is the *homo oeconomicus* an ideal type in Max Weber's sense. Classical economics did not want to exalt a certain human type—for example, the English businessman of the nineteenth century, or the businessman in general. As genuine praxeology—and economics is a branch of praxeology—it aspired to a universal, timeless understanding that would embrace all economic action. (That it could not succeed in this endeavor is another matter.) But this is something that can only be indicated here. To make it evident, it would have to be shown that an ideal type cannot be constructed on the basis of a formal, theoretical science like praxeology, but only on the basis of concrete historical data.[17] However, such a task goes beyond the scope of this discussion.

By means of its subjectivism the modern theory becomes objective science. It does not pass judgment on action, but takes it exactly as it is; and it explains market phenomena not on the basis of "right" action, but on the basis of given action. It does not seek to explain the exchange ratios that would exist on the supposition that men are governed exclusively by certain motives and that other motives, which do in fact govern them, have no effect. It wants to comprehend the formation of the exchange ratios that actually appear in the market.

The determination of the prices of what Menger calls "imaginary goods" follows the same laws as that of "real goods." Böhm-Bawerk's "other motives" cause no fundamental alteration in the market process; they change only the data.

It was necessary to expressly point out these mistakes of Menger and Böhm-Bawerk (which, as we have noted above, are also encountered in other authors) in order to avoid misinterpretations of the theory. But all the more emphatically must it be stated that neither Menger nor Böhm-Bawerk allowed themselves to be misled in any way in the development of their theory of price determination and imputation by

---

[17] Mises' *Epistemological Problems of Economics,* pp. 75 ff.

consideration for the differences in the motives that lie behind the action of the parties on the market. The assertions that were designated as erroneous in the preceding remarks did not in the least detract from the general merit of their work: to explain the determination of prices in terms of the subjective theory of value.

On the Development of the Subjective Theory of Value*

by Ludwig von Mises

1. The Delimitation of the "Economic"

Investigation concerning the money prices of goods and services constituted the historical starting point of the reflections that led to the development of economic theory. What first opened the way to success in these inquiries was the observation that money plays "merely" an intermediary role and that through its interposition goods and services are, in the last analysis, exchanged against goods and services. This discovery led to the further realization that the theory of direct exchange, which makes use of the fiction that all acts of exchange are conducted without the intervention of any medium, must be given logical priority over the theory of money and credit, i.e., the theory of indirect exchange, which is effected by means of money.

Still further possibilities were disclosed when it was realized that acts of interpersonal exchange are not essentially different from those which the individual makes within his own household without reaching beyond it into the social sphere. Hence, every allocation of goods—even those in the processes of production—is an exchange, and consequently the basic law of economic action can be comprehended also in the conduct of the isolated farmer. Thus, the foundation was laid for the first correct formulation and satisfactory solution of the problem of the delimitation of "economic" action from "noneconomic" action.

This problem had been approached previously in two different ways, each of which necessarily rendered its solution considerably more difficult. Classical economics had not succeeded in overcoming the difficulties posed by the apparent paradox of value. It had to construct its theory of value and price formation on the basis of exchange

* Included in *Grundprobleme der Nationalökonomie* (1933). [English translation: *Epistemological Problems of Economics*. Translated from the German by George Reisman. (Princeton, N.J.: D. Van Nostrand, 1960; New York: New York University Press, 1981)]. This chapter reprinted here by permission.

value and to start from the action of the businessman, because it was not able to base its system on the valuations of the marginal consumers. The specific conduct of the businessman is directed toward the attainment of the greatest possible monetary profit. Since the Classical economists beheld in this phenomenon the essence of economic conduct, they had to distinguish accordingly between "economic" and "noneconomic" action. As soon as the transition was made to the subjective theory of value, this distinction, because it contradicts the basic thought of the whole system, could not but prove totally unserviceable and indeed nothing short of absurd. Of course, it took a long time before it was recognized as such.

If the distinction between the "economic" and the "noneconomic" proved untenable when formulated in terms of the motives and immediate goals of the actor, the attempt to base it on differences among the objects of action fared no better. Material things of the external world are exchanged not only against other things of this kind; they are exchanged also against other—"immaterial—goods like honor, fame and recognition. If one wishes to remove these actions from the province of the "economic," then a new difficulty arises. For a great many of the acts in which material goods are exchanged serve one or both parties to the transaction merely as a preliminary means for the attainment of such "immaterial" satisfactions. However, every attempt to draw a sharp distinction here necessarily led to barren scholastic discussions which entangled themselves in immanent contradictions—discussions such as the successors of the Classical economists devoted to the related endeavors to delimit the concepts of a "good" and "productivity." But even if one wishes to disregard this problem completely, one could not ignore the fact that human action exhibits an indissoluble homogeneity and that action involving the exchange of material goods against immaterial goods differs in no significant respect from action involving the exchange of material goods alone.

Two propositions follow from the subjective theory of value that make a precise separation between the "economic" and the "noneconomic," such as the older economics sought, appear impracticable. First, there is the realization that the economic principle is the fundamental principle of all rational action, and not just a particular feature of a certain kind of rational action. All rational action is therefore an act of economizing. Secondly, there is a realization that every conscious, i.e., meaningful, action is rational. Only the ultimate goals—the values or ends—at which action aims are beyond rationality and, indeed, always and without exception must be. It was no longer compatible with subjectivism to equate "rational" and "irrational" with "objectively practical" and "objectively impractical." It was no longer permissible to contrast "correct" action as "rational" to "incorrect" action, i.e., action diverted through misunderstanding, ignorance, or negligence from employing the best means available to attain the ends sought. Nor was it henceforth possible to call an action irrational in which values like honor, piety, or political goals are taken into consideration. Max Weber's attempt to separate rational action from other action on the basis of such distinctions was the last of its kind. It was necessarily doomed to failure.[1]

If, however, all conscious conduct is an act of rational economizing, then one must be able to exhibit the fundamental economic categories involved in every action, even in action that is called "noneconomic" in popular usage. And, in fact, it is not difficult to point out in every conceivable human action—that is, conscious action—the fundamental categories of catallactics, namely, value, good, exchange, price, and costs. Not only does the science of ethics show this, but even everyday popular usage gives us ample demonstrations of it. One has only to consider, for example, how, outside the domain customarily designated as that of science, terms and phrases are used that have these categories as their specific denotation.

2. Preferring as the Basic Element in Human Conduct

All conscious conduct on the part of men involves preferring an A to a B. It is an act of choice between two alternative possibilities that offer themselves. Only these acts of choice, these inner decisions that operate upon the external world, are our data. We comprehend their meaning by constructing the concept of importance. If an individual prefers A to B, we say that, at the moment of the act of choice, A appeared more important to him (more valuable, more desirable) than B.

We are also wont to say that the need for A was more urgent than the need for B. This is a mode of expression that, under certain circumstances, may be quite expedient. But as an hypostatization of what was to be explained, it became a source of serious misunderstandings. It was forgotten that we are able to infer the need only from the action. Hence, the idea of an action not in conformity with needs is absurd. As soon as one attempts to distinguish between the need and the action and makes the need the criterion for judging the action, one leaves the domain of theoretical science, with its neutrality in regard to value

---

[1] See Mises' *Epistemological Problems,* pp. 82 ff.

judgments. It is necessary to recall here that we are dealing with the theory of action, not with psychology, and certainly not with a system of norms, which has the task of differentiating between good and evil or between value and worthlessness. Our data are actions and conduct. It may be left undecided how far and in what way our science needs to concern itself with what lies behind them, that is, with actual valuations and volitions. For there can be no doubt that its subject matter is given action and only given action. Action that ought to be, but is not, does not come within its purview.

This best becomes clear to us if we consider the task of catallactics. Catallactics has to explain how market prices arise from the action of parties to the exchange of goods. It has to explain market prices as they are, not as they should be. If one wishes to do justice to this task, then in no way may one distinguish between "economic" and "noneconomic" grounds of price determination or limit oneself to constructing a theory that would apply only to a world that does not exist. In Böhm-Bawerk's famous example of the planter's five sacks of grain, there is no question of a rank order of objective correctness, but of a rank order of subjective desires.

The boundary that separates the economic from the noneconomic is not to be sought within the compass of rational action. It coincides with the line that separates action from nonaction. Action takes place only where decisions are to be made, where the necessity exists of choosing between possible goals, because all goals either cannot be achieved at all or not at the same time. Men act because they are affected by the flux of time. They are therefore not indifferent to the passage of time. They act because they are not fully satisfied and satiated and because by acting they are able to enhance the degree of their satisfaction. Where these conditions are not present—as in the case of "free" goods, for example—action does not take place.

3. Eudaemonism and the Theory of Value

The most troublesome misunderstandings with which the history of philosophical thought has been plagued concern the terms "pleasure" and "pain." These misconceptions have been carried over into the literature of sociology [praxeology] and economics and have caused harm there too.

Before the introduction of this pair of concepts, ethics was a doctrine of what ought to be. It sought to establish the goals that man should adopt. The realization that man seeks satisfaction by acts both of commission and of omission opened the only path that can lead to a science of human action. If Epicurus sees in ἀταραξία [complete peace of mind] the final goal of action, we can behold in it, if we wish, the state of complete satisfaction and freedom from desire at which human action aims without ever being able to attain it. Crude materialistic thinking seeks to circumscribe it in visions of Paradise and Cockaigne. Whether this construction may, in fact, be placed on Epicurus' words remains, of course, uncertain, in view of the paucity of what has been handed down of his writings.

Doubtless it did not happen altogether without the fault of Epicurus and his school that the concepts of pleasure and pain were taken in the narrowest and coarsely materialistic sense when one wanted to misconstrue the ideas of hedonism and eudaemonism. And they were not only misconstrued; they were deliberately misrepresented, caricatured, derided, and ridiculed. Not until the seventeenth century did appreciation of the teachings of Epicurus again begin to be shown. On the foundations provided by it arose modern utilitarianism, which for its part soon had to contend anew with the same misrepresentations on the part of its opponents that had confronted its ancient forerunner. Hedonism, eudaemonism, and utilitarianism were condemned and outlawed, and whoever did not wish to run the risk of making the whole world his enemy had to be scrupulously intent upon avoiding the suspicion that he inclined toward these heretical doctrines. This must be kept in mind if one wants to understand why many economists went to great pains to deny the connection between their teachings and those of utilitarianism.

Even Böhm-Bawerk thought that he had to defend himself against the reproach of hedonism. The heart of this defense consists in his statement that he had expressly called attention already in the first exposition of his theory of value to his use of the word "well-being" in its broadest sense, in which it "embraces not only the self-centered interests of a subject, but everything that seems to him worth aiming at."[2] Böhm-Bawerk did not see that in saying this he was adopting the same purely formal view of the character of the basic eudaemonistic concepts of pleasure and pain—treating them as indifferent to content—that all advanced utilitarians have held. One need only compare with the words quoted from Böhm-Bawerk, the following dictum of Jacobi:

> We originally want or desire an object not because it is agreeable or good, but we call it agreeable or good because we want

---

[2] Böhm-Bawerk, *Kapital und Kapitalzins*, II, vol. 1, p. 236n. [English translation, *Capital and Interest* II, 188 note 70, p. 429].

or desire it; and we do this because our sensuous or supersen-
suous nature so requires. There is, thus, no basis for recognizing what is good and worth wishing for outside of the faculty
of desiring—i.e., the original desire and the wish themselves.[3]

We need not go further into the fact that every ethic, no matter how
strict an opponent of eudaemonism it may at first appear to be, must
somehow clandestinely smuggle the idea of happiness into its system.
As Böhm-Bawerk has shown, the case is no different with "ethical" economics.[4] That the concepts of pleasure and pain contain no reference to
the content of what is aimed at, ought, indeed, scarcely to be still open
to misunderstanding.

Once this fact is established, the ground is removed from all the
objections advanced by "ethical" economics and related schools. There
may be men who aim at different ends, from those of the men we know,
but as long as there are men—that is, as long as they do not merely
graze like animals or vegetate like plants, but act because they seek to
attain goals—they will necessarily always be subject to the logic of
action, the investigation of which is the task of our science. In this sense
that science is universally human, and not limited by nationality,
bound to a particular time, or contingent upon any social class. In this
sense too it is logically prior to all historical and descriptive research.

4. Economics and Psychology

The expression "Psychological School" is frequently employed as a
designation of modern subjectivist economics. Occasionally too the difference in method that exists between the School of Lausanne and the
Austrian school is indicated by attributing to the latter the "psychological" method. It is not surprising that the idea of economics as always a
branch of psychology or applied psychology should have arisen from
such a habit of speech. Today, neither these misunderstandings nor
their employment in the struggle carried on over the Austrian school
are of anything more than historical and literary interest.

Nevertheless, the relationship of economics to psychology is still
problematical. The position due Gossen's law of the satiation of wants
yet remains to be clarified.

Perhaps it will be useful first to look at the route that had to be tra-

---

[3] According to Fr. A. Schmid, quoted by Jodl, *Geschichte der Ethik* (2nd ed.), II, 661.

[4] See Böhm-Bawerk's comments on Schmoller, *op. cit.*, p. 239n. [English translation,
II, 190, p. 429–430 n.71]. On Vierkandt, see Mises' *Epistemological Problems*, p. 55.

versed in order to arrive at the modern treatment of the problem of price formation. In this way we shall best succeed in assigning Gossen's first law its position in the system, which is different from the one it occupied when it was first discovered.

The earlier attempts to investigate the laws of price determination foundered on the universalist [collectivist] approach which was accepted under the sway of conceptual realism [the theory that abstract universals are real and independent of their parts]. The importance which attached to nominalistic thought [doctrine that man can only conceive of particular or individual things, persons, events] in antiquity, in the Middle Ages, and at the beginning of the modern era should not, of course, be underestimated. Nevertheless, it is certain that almost all attempts to comprehend social phenomena were at first undertaken on the basis of the principle of universalism. And on this basis they could not but fail hopelessly. Whoever wanted to explain prices saw, on the one hand, mankind, the state, and the corporative unit, and, on the other, classes of goods here and money there. They were also nominalistic attempts to solve these problems, and to them we owe the beginnings of the subjective theory of value. However, they were repeatedly stifled by the prestige of the prevailing conceptual realism.

Only the disintegration of the universalistic mentality brought about by the methodological individualism of the seventeenth and eighteenth centuries cleared the way for the development of a scientific catallactics. It was seen that on the market it is not mankind, the state, or the corporative unit that acts, but individual men and groups of men, and that *their* valuations and *their* actions are decisive, not those of abstract collectivities. To recognize the relationship between valuation and use value and thus cope with the paradox of value, one had to realize that not classes of goods are involved in exchange, but concrete units of goods. This discovery signaled nothing less than a Copernican revolution in social science. Yet it required more than another hundred years for the step to be taken. This is a short span of time if we view the matter from the standpoint of world history and if we adequately appreciate the difficulties involved. But in the history of our science precisely this period acquired a special importance, inasmuch as it was during this time that the marvelous structure of Ricardo's system was first elaborated. In spite of the serious misunderstanding on which it was constructed, it became so fruitful that it rightly bears the designation "Classical."

The step that leads from Classical to modern economics is the realization that classes of goods in the abstract are never exchanged and valued, but always only concrete units of a class of goods. If I buy or sell *one* loaf of bread, I do not take into consideration what "bread" is worth to mankind, or what all the bread currently available is worth, or what 10,000 loaves of bread are worth, but only the worth of the *one* loaf in question. This realization is not a deduction from Gossen's first law. It is attained through reflection on the essence of our action; or, expressed differently, the experience of our action makes any other supposition impossible for our thought.

We derive the law of the satiation of wants from this proposition and from the further realization, which is obtained by reflecting upon our action that, in our scales of importance, we order individual units of goods, not according to the classes of goods to which they belong or the classes of wants which they satisfy, but according to the concrete emergence of wants; that is to say, before one class of wants is fully satisfied we already proceed to the satisfaction of individual wants of other classes that we would not satisfy if one or several wants of the first class had not previously been satisfied.

Therefore, from our standpoint, Gossen's law has nothing to do with psychology. It is deduced by economics from reflections that are not of a psychological nature. The psychological law of satiation is independent of our law, though understandably in harmony with it inasmuch as both refer to the same state of affairs. What distinguishes the two is the difference of method by which they have been arrived at. Psychology and economics are differentiated by their methods of viewing man.

To be sure, Bentham, who may be numbered among the greatest theorists of social science and who stood at the peak of the economics of his time, arrived at our law by way of psychology and was unable to make any application of it to economics; and in Gossen's exposition it appeared as a psychological law, on which economic theory was then constructed. But these facts in no way invalidate the distinction that we have drawn between the laws of economics and those of psychology. Bentham's great intellect did not serve one science only. We do not know how Gossen arrived at his cognition, and it is a matter of indifference as far as answering our question is concerned. The investigation of the way in which this or that truth was first discovered is important only for history, not for a theoretical science. It is, of course, obvious that the position that Gossen then assigned the law in his system can have no authoritative standing in our view. And everyone knows that Menger, Jevons, and Walras did not arrive at the resolution of the paradox of value by way of Gossen's law.

5. Economics and Technology

The system of economic theory is independent of all other sciences as well as of psychology. This is true also of its relationship to technology. By way of illustration we shall demonstrate this in the case of the law of returns.

Even historically the law of returns did not originate in technology, but in reflections on economics. One interpreted the fact that the farmer who wants to produce more also wants to extend the area under cultivation and that in doing so he even makes use of poorer soil. If the law of returns did not hold true, it could not be explained how there can be such a thing as "land hunger." Land would have to be a free good. The natural sciences, in developing a theory of agriculture, were unable either to substantiate or to confute these reflections "empirically." The experience that it took as its starting point was the fact that arable land is treated as an economic good.[5] It is obvious that here too economics and the natural sciences must meet on common ground.

One could not help finally expanding the law of diminishing returns on the cultivation of land into a general law of returns. If a good of higher order is treated as an economic good, then the law of returns—increasing returns up to a certain point, and beyond that point diminishing returns—must hold true of this good. Simple reflection shows that a good of higher order of which the law of returns did not hold true could never be regarded as an economic good: it would be indifferent to us whether larger or smaller quantities of this good were available.

The law of population is a special case of the law of returns. If the increase in the number of workers were always to bring about a proportional increase in returns, then the increase in the means of support would keep pace with the increase in population.

Whoever maintains, like Henry George, Franz Oppenheimer, and others, that the law of population is without practical importance assumes that hand in hand with every increase in population beyond the optimum necessarily go changes in technology or in the social division of labor such that at least no decrease in returns takes place per capita of the total population and perhaps even an increase in returns is thereby brought about. There is no proof for this assumption.

---

[5] Cf. Böhm-Bawerk, *Gesammelte Schriften*, ed. by F. X. Weiss (Vienna, 1924), I, 193ff.

6. Monetary Calculation and the "Economic in the Narrower Sense"

All action aims at results and takes on meaning only in relation to results. The preferring and setting aside that are involved in action take as their standard the importance of the anticipated result for the well-being of the actor. Whatever directly serves well-being is, without difficulty, given a rank in accordance with its importance, and this provides the rank order in which the goals of action stand at any given moment. How far it is possible to bring the relatively remote prerequisites of well-being into this rank order without resorting to more complicated processes of thought depends on the intelligence of the individual. It is certain, however, that even for the most gifted person the difficulties of weighing means and ends becomes insurmountable as soon as one goes beyond the simplest processes of production involving only a short period of time and few intermediary steps. Capitalistic production—in Böhm-Bawerk's sense, not in that of the Marxists—requires above all else the tool of economic calculation, through which expenditures of goods and of labor of different kinds become comparable. Those who act must be capable of recognizing which path leads to the goal aimed at with the least expenditure of means. This is the function of monetary calculation.

Money—that is, the generally used medium of exchange—thus becomes an indispensable mental prerequisite of any action that undertakes to conduct relatively long-range processes of production. Without the aid of monetary calculation, bookkeeping, and the computation of profit and loss in terms of money, technology would have had to confine itself to the simplest, and therefore the least productive, methods. If today economic calculation were again to disappear from production—as the result, for example, of the attainment of full socialization—then the whole structure of capitalistic production would be transformed within the shortest time into a desolate chaos, from which there could be no other way out than reversion to the economic condition of the most primitive cultures. Inasmuch as money prices of the means of production can be determined only in a social order in which they are privately owned, the proof of the impracticability of socialism necessarily follows.

From the standpoint of both politics and history, this proof is certainly the most important discovery made by economic theory. Its practical significance can scarcely be overestimated. It alone gives us the basis for pronouncing a final political judgment on all kinds of socialism, communism, and planned economies; and it alone will enable future historians to understand how it came about that the victory of the socialist movement did not lead to the creation of the socialist order of society. Here we need not go into this further. We must consider the problem of monetary calculation in another respect, namely, in its importance for the separation of action "economic in the narrower sense" from other action.

The characteristic feature of the mental tool provided by monetary calculation is responsible for the fact that the sphere in which it is employed appears to us as a special province within the wider domain of all action. In everyday, popular usage the sphere of the economic extends as far as monetary calculations are possible. Whatever goes beyond this is called the noneconomic sphere. We cannot acquiesce in this usage when it treats economic and noneconomic action as heterogeneous. We have seen that such a separation is misleading. However, the very fact that we see in economic calculation in terms of money the most important and, indeed, the indispensable mental tool of long-range production makes a terminological separation between these two spheres appear expedient to us. In the light of the comments above, we must reject the terms "economic" and "noneconomic" or "uneconomic," but we can accept the terms "economic in the narrower sense" and "economic in the broader sense," provided one does not want to interpret them as indicating a difference in the scope of rational and economic action.

(We may remark incidentally that monetary calculation is no more a "function" of money than astronomical navigation is a "function" of the stars.)

Economic calculation is either the calculation of future possibilities as the basis for the decisions that guide action, or the subsequent ascertainment of the results, i.e., the computation of profit and loss. In no respect can it be called "perfect." One of the tasks of the theory of indirect exchange (the theory of money and credit) consists precisely in showing the imperfection—or, more correctly, the limits—of what this method is capable of. Nonetheless, it is the only method available to a society based on the division of labor when it wants to compare the input and the output of its production processes. All attempts on the part of the apologists of socialism to concoct a scheme for a "socialist economic calculation" must, therefore, necessarily fail.

7. Exchange Ratios and the Limits of Monetary Calculation

The money prices of goods and services that we are able to ascertain are the ratios in which these goods and services were exchanged against money at a given moment of the relatively recent or remote past. These ratios are always past; they always belong to history. They correspond to a market situation that is not the market situation of today.

Economic calculation is able to utilize to a certain extent the prices of the market because, as a rule, they do not shift so rapidly that such calculation could be essentially falsified by it. Moreover, certain deviations and changes can be appraised with so close an approximation to what really takes place later that action—or "practice"— is able to manage quite well with monetary calculation notwithstanding all its deficiencies.

It cannot be emphasized strongly enough, however, that this practice is always the practice of the acting individual who wants to discover the result of his particular action (as far as it does not go beyond the orbit of the economic in the narrower sense). It always occurs within the framework of a social order based on private ownership of the means of production. It is the entrepreneur's calculation of profitability. It can never become anything more.

Therefore, it is absurd to want to apply the elements of this calculation to other problems other than those confronting the individual actor. One may not extend them to *res extra commercium.* One may not attempt by means of them to include more than the sphere of the economic in the narrower sense. However, this is precisely what is attempted by those who undertake to ascertain the monetary value of human life, social institutions, national wealth, cultural ideals, or the like, or who enter upon highly sophisticated investigations to determine how exchange ratios of the relatively recent, not to mention the remote, past could be expressed in terms of "our money."

It is no less absurd to fall back upon monetary calculation when one seeks to contrast the productivity of action to its profitability. In comparing the profitability and the productivity of action, one compares the result as it appears to the individual acting within the social order of capitalism with the result as it would appear to the central director of an imaginary socialist community. (We may ignore for the sake of argument the fact that he would be completely unable to carry out such calculations.)

The height of conceptual confusion is reached when one tries to bring calculation to bear upon the problem of what is called the "social maximization of profit." Here the connection with the individual's calculation of profitability is intentionally abandoned in order to go beyond the "individualistic" and "atomistic" and arrive at "social" findings. And again one fails to see and will not see that the system of calculation is inseparably connected with the individual's calculation of profitability.

Monetary calculation is not the calculation, and certainly not the measurement, of value. Its basis is the comparison of the more important and the less important. It is an ordering according to rank, an act of grading (Čuhel) and not an act of measuring. It was a mistake to search for a measure of the value of goods. In the last analysis, economic calculation does not rest on the measurement of values, but on their arrangement in an order of rank.

8. Changes in the Data

The universally valid theory of economic action is necessarily formal. Its material content consists of the data of human circumstances, which evoke action in the individual case: the goals at which men aim and the means by which they seek to attain them.[6]

The equilibrium position of the market corresponds to the specific configuration of the data. If the data change, then the equilibrium position also shifts. We grasp the effect of changes in the data by means of our theory. With its help we can also predict the quality—or, rather, the direction—of the changes that, *ceteris paribus*, must follow definite changes in the data. From the known extent of changes in the latter, we are unable to predetermine quantitatively what these consequent changes will be. For changes in external conditions must, in order to influence action, be translated into volitions that move men from within. We know nothing about this process. Even materialism, which professes to have solved the problem of the relation between the psychical and the physical by means of the famous simple formula that thinking stands in the same relationship to the brain as gall does to the bladder, has not even undertaken the attempt to establish a constant relationship between definite external events, which are quantitatively and qualitatively discernible, and thoughts and volitions.

All the endeavors that have been and are being devoted to the construction of a quantitative theory of catallactics must, therefore, come to grief. All that can be accomplished in this area is economic history. It can never go beyond the unique and the nonrepeatable; it can never acquire universal validity.[7]

9. The Role of Time in the Economy

Classical economics distinguished three factors of production: land, labor, and capital. Inasmuch as capital can be resolved into land

---

[6] *Cf.* the fruitful investigations of Strigl: *Die ökonomischen Kategorien und die Organisation der Wirtschaft* (Jena, 1923).

[7] This is also true, for example, of the attempts of Moore in particular (*Synthetic Economics*, New York, 1929) *Cf.* the critique by Ricci, *Zeitschrift für Sozialpolitik*, I, 694ff.

and labor, two factors remain: labor and the "conditions of well-being" made available by nature. If consumption goods are disregarded, these alone, according to the view to be found in the older literature, are the objects of economizing.

The Classical economists, whose attention was directed above all to the conduct of the businessman, could not observe that time too is economized. An account for "time" does not appear in the business-man's books. No price is paid for it on markets. That it is, nevertheless, taken into consideration in every exchange could not be seen from the standpoint of an objectivistic theory of value, nor could one be led to this realization by reflection on the popular precept contained in the saying, "Time is money." It was one of the great achievements of Jevons and Böhm-Bawerk that, in carrying on the work of Bentham and Rae, they assigned the element of time its proper place in the system of economic theory.

The Classical economists failed to recognize the essential importance of time, which manifests its effect directly or indirectly in every exchange. They did not see that action always distinguishes between the present and the future—between present goods and future goods. Yet the time differential is important for the economy in still another respect. All changes in the data can make themselves felt only over a period of time. A longer or a shorter period must elapse before the new state of equilibrium, in accordance with the emergence of the new datum, can be reached. The static—or, as the Classical economists called it, the natural—price is not reached immediately, but only after some time has passed. In the interim, deviations ensue that become the source of special profits and losses. The Classical economists and their epigones not only did not fail to recognize this fact; on the contrary, they occasionally overestimated its importance. The modern theory too has paid special attention to it. This is true above all of the theory of indirect exchange. The theory of changes in the purchasing power of money and of their concomitant social consequences is based entirely on this fact. A short while ago, in a spirit of remarkable terminological and scholastic conscientiousness, an attempt was made to deny to the circulation credit theory of the trade cycle its customary name, viz., the monetary theory of crises, on the ground that it is constructed on the basis of a "time lag."[8]

As has been stated, economic theory has failed to see the impor-

---

[8] *Cf.* Burchardt, "Entwicklungsgeschichte der monetären Konjunkturtheorie," *Weltwirtschaftliches Archiv* XXVIII, 140; Löwe, "Über den Einfluss monetärer Faktoren auf den Konjunkturzyclus," *Schriften des Vereins für Sozialpolitik*, CLXXIII, 362.

tance of the fact that a shorter or a longer period of time must go by before the equilibrium of the market, once it has been disturbed by emergence of new data, can again be established. This assertion would never have been made if, for political reasons, repeated attempts had not been made to embarrass the discussion of economic questions with irrelevant objections. The defenders of interventionism have occasionally attempted to confront the arguments of the critics of this policy— arguments supported by the irrefutable deductions of economics— with the alleged fact that the propositions of economics hold true only in the long run. Therefore, it was maintained, the ineluctable conclusion that interventionist measures are senseless and inexpedient cannot yet be drawn. It would exceed the scope of this treatise to examine what force this argument has in the dispute over interventionism. It is sufficient here to point out that the liberal doctrine provides a direct, and not merely an indirect, demonstration of the senselessness and inexpediency of interventionism and that the accomplishments of interventions can be refuted only by pointing to interventionist measures that are not effective and that, in fact, bring about effects that run counter to the intentions of those who have recourse to them.

10. "Resistances"

The economist is often prone to look to mechanics as a model for his own work. Instead of treating the problems posed by his science with the means appropriate to them, he fetches a metaphor from mechanics, which he puts in place of a solution. In this way the idea arose that the laws of catallactics hold true only ideally, i.e., on the assumption that men act in a vacuum, as it were. But, of course, in life everything happens quite differently. In life there are "frictional resistances" of all kinds, which are responsible for the fact that the outcome of our action is different from what the laws would lead one to expect. From the very outset no way was seen in which these resistances could be exactly measured or, indeed, fully comprehended even qualitatively. So one had to resign oneself to admitting that economics has but slight value both for the cognition of the relationships of our life in society and for actual practice. And, of course, all those who rejected economic science for political and related reasons—all the etatists, the socialists, and the interventionists—joyfully agree.

Once the distinction between economic and noneconomic action is abandoned, it is not difficult to see that in all cases of "resistance" what is involved is the concrete data of economizing, which the theory comprehends fully.

For example, we deduce from our theory that when the price of a commodity rises, its production will be increased. However, if the expansion of production necessitates new investment of capital, which requires considerable time, a certain period of time will elapse before the price rise brings about an increase in supply. And if the new investment required to expand production would commit capital in such a way that conversion of invested capital goods in another branch of production is altogether impossible or, if possible, is possible only at the cost of heavy losses, and if one is of the opinion that the price of the commodity will soon drop again, then the expansion of production does not take place at all. In the whole process there is nothing that the theory could not immediately explain to us.

Therefore, it is also incorrect to make the assertion that the propositions of the theory hold true only in the case of perfectly free competition. This objection must appear all the more remarkable as one could sooner assert that the modern theory of price determination has devoted too much attention to the problem of monopoly price. It certainly stands to reason that the propositions of the theory should first be examined with respect to the simplest case. Hence, it is not a legitimate criticism of economic theory that, in the investigation of competitive prices, it generally starts from the assumption that all goods are indefinitely divisible, that no obstacles stand in the way of the mobility of capital and labor, that no errors are made, etc. The subsequent dropping of these elementary assumptions one by one then affords no difficulty.

It is true that the Classical economists inferred from their inquiry into the problems of catallactics that, as far as practical economic policy is concerned, all the obstacles that interventionism places in the path of competition not only diminish the quantity and value of the total production, but cannot lead to the goals that one seeks to attain by such measures. The investigations that modern economics has devoted to the same problem lead to the identical conclusion. The fact that the politician must draw from the teachings of economic theory the inference that no obstacles should be placed in the way of competition unless one has the intention of lowering productivity does not imply that the theory is unable to cope with the "fettered" economy and "frictional resistances."

11. Costs

By costs Classical economics understood a quantity of goods and labor. From the standpoint of the modern theory, cost is the importance of the next most urgent want that can now no longer be satisfied. This conception of cost is clearly expressed outside the orbit of the economic in the narrower sense in a statement like the following, for example: The work involved in preparing for the examination cost me (i.e., prevented) my trip to Italy. Had I not had to study for the examination, I should have taken a trip to Italy.

Only if one employs this concept of cost does one realize the importance that attaches to profitability. The fact that production is discontinued beyond the point at which it ceases to be profitable means that production takes place only as far as the goods of higher order and the labor required to produce one commodity are not more urgently needed to produce other commodities. This observation shows how unwarranted is the popular practice of objecting to the limitation of production to profitable undertakings without also mentioning those enterprises that would have to be discontinued if others were maintained beyond the point of profitability.

The same observation also disposes of the assertion, made repeatedly, that the subjective theory of value does justice only to the private aspect of price formation and not to its economic implications for society as well. On the contrary, one could turn this objection around and argue that whoever traces the determination of prices to the costs of production alone does not go beyond the outlook of the individual businessman or producer. Only the reduction of the concept of cost to its ultimate basis, as carried out by the theory of marginal utility, brings the social aspect of economic action entirely into view.

Within the field of modern economics the Austrian school has shown its superiority to the school of Lausanne and the schools related to the latter, which favor mathematical formulations, by clarifying the causal relationship between value and cost, while at the same time eschewing the concept of function, which in our science is misleading. The Austrian school must also be credited with not having stopped at the concept of cost but, on the contrary, with carrying on its investigations to the point where it is able to trace back even this concept to subjective value judgments.

Once one has correctly grasped the position of the concept of cost within the framework of modern science, one will have no difficulty in seeing that economics exhibits a continuity of development no less definite than that presented by the history of other sciences. The popular assertion that there are various schools of economics whose theories have nothing in common and that every economist begins by destroying the work of his predecessors in order to construct his own theory on its ruins is no more true than the other legends that the proponents of historicism, socialism, and interventionism have spread about economics. In fact, a straight line leads from the system of the Classical economists to the subjectivist economics of the present. The latter is erected not on the ruins, but on the foundations, of the Classical system. Modern economics has taken from its predecessor the best that it was able to offer. Without the work that the Classical economists accomplished, it would not have been possible to advance to the discoveries of the modern school. Indeed, it was the uncertainties of the objectivistic school itself that necessarily led to the solutions offered by subjectivism. No work that had been devoted to the problem was done in vain. Everything that appears to those who have come afterward as a blind alley or at least as a wrong turning on the way toward a solution was necessary in order to exhaust all possibilities and to explore and think through to its logical conclusion every consideration to which the problems might lead.

The Epistemological Problems*

by Ludwig von Mises

The Formal and Aprioristic Character of Praxeology

A fashionable tendency in contemporary philosophy is to deny the existence of any a priori knowledge. All human knowledge, it is contended, is derived from experience. This attitude can easily be understood as an excessive reaction against the extravagances of theology and a spurious philosophy of history and of nature. Metaphysicians were eager to discover by intuition moral precepts, the meaning of historical evolution, the properties of soul and matter, and the laws governing physical, chemical, and physiological events. Their volatile speculations manifested a blithe disregard for matter-of-fact knowledge. They were convinced that, without reference to experience, reason could explain all things and answer all questions.

The modern natural sciences owe their success to the method of observation and experiment. There is no doubt that empiricism and pragmatism are right as far as they merely describe the procedures of the natural sciences. But it is no less certain that they are entirely wrong in their endeavors to reject any kind of a priori knowledge and to characterize logic, mathematics, and praxeology either as empirical and experimental disciplines or as mere tautologies. With regard to praxeology the errors of the philosophers are due to their complete ignorance of economics[1] and very often to their shockingly insufficient knowledge of history. In the eyes of the philosopher the treatment of philosophical issues is a sublime and noble vocation which must not be put

---

* Reprinted with permission from *Human Action*. Chapter II.

[1] Hardly any philosopher had a more universal familiarity with various branches of contemporary knowledge than Bergson. Yet a casual remark in his last great book clearly proves that Bergson was completely ignorant of the fundamental theorem of the modern theory of value and exchange. Speaking of exchange he remarks "I'on ne peut le pratiquer sans s'être demandé si les deux objets échangés sont bien de même valeur, c'est-à-dire échangeables contre un même troisième" [one cannot barter without first finding out if the two objects exchanged are equal in value, that is to say exchangeable for a definite third object]. (*Les Deux Sources de la morale et de la religion* [Paris, 1932], p. 68.)

137

upon the low level of other gainful employments. The professor resents the fact that he derives an income from philosophizing; he is offended by the thought that he earns money like the artisan and the farm hand. Monetary matters are mean things, and the philosopher investigating the eminent problems of truth and absolute eternal values should not soil his mind by paying attention to problems of economics.

The problem of whether there are or whether there are not a priori elements of thought—i.e., necessary and ineluctable intellectual conditions of thinking, anterior to any actual instance of conception and experience—must not be confused with the genetic problem of how man acquired his characteristically human mental ability. These ancestors were endowed with some potentiality which in the course of ages of evolution converted them into reasonable beings. This transformation was achieved by the influence of a changing cosmic environment operating upon succeeding generations. Hence the empiricist concludes that the fundamental principles of reasoning are an outcome of experience and represent an adaptation of man to the conditions of his environment.

This idea leads, when consistently followed, to the further conclusion that there were between our prehuman ancestors and homo sapiens various intermediate stages. There were beings which, although not yet equipped with the human faculty of reason, were endowed with some rudimentary elements of ratiocination. Theirs was not yet a logical mind, but a prelogical (or rather imperfectly logical) mind. Their desultory and defective logical functions evolved step by step from the prelogical state toward the logical state. Reason, intellect, and logic are historical phenomena. There is a history of logic as there is a history of technology. Nothing suggests that logic as we know it is the last and final state of intellectual evolution. Human logic is a historical phase between prehuman nonlogic on the one hand and superhuman logic on the other hand. Reason and mind, the human beings' most efficacious equipment in their struggle for survival, are embedded in the continuous flow of zoological events. They are neither eternal nor unchangeable. They are transitory.

Furthermore, there is no doubt that every human being repeats in his personal evolution not only the physiological metamorphosis from a simple cell into a highly complicated mammal organism but no less the spiritual metamorphosis from a purely vegetative and animal existence into a reasonable mind. This transformation is not completed in the prenatal life of the embryo, but only later when the newborn child step by step awakens to human consciousness. Thus every man in his early youth, starting from the depths of darkness, proceeds through various states of the mind's logical structure.

Then there is the case of the animals. We are fully aware of the unbridgeable gulf separating our reason from the reactive processes of their brains and nerves. But at the same time we divine that forces are desperately struggling in them toward the light of comprehension. They are like prisoners anxious to break out from the doom of eternal darkness and inescapable automatism. We feel with them because we ourselves are in a similar position: pressing in vain against the limitation of our intellectual apparatus, striving unavailingly after unattainable perfect cognition.

But the problem of the a priori is of a different character. It does not deal with the problem of how consciousness and reason have emerged. It refers to the essential and necessary character of the logical structure of the human mind.

The fundamental logical relations are not subject to proof or disproof. Every attempt to prove them must presuppose their validity. It is impossible to explain them to a being who would not possess them on his own account. Efforts to define them according to the rules of definition must fail. They are primary propositions antecedent to any nominal or real definition. They are ultimate unanalyzable categories. The human mind is utterly incapable of imagining logical categories at variance with them. No matter how they may appear to superhuman beings, they are for man inescapable and absolutely necessary. They are the indispensable prerequisite of perception, apperception, and experience.

They are no less an indispensable prerequisite of memory. There is a tendency in the natural sciences to describe memory as an instance of a more general phenomenon. Every living organism conserves the effects of earlier stimulation, and the present state of inorganic matter is shaped by the effects of all the influences to which it was exposed in the past. The present state of the universe is the product of its past. We may, therefore, in a loose metaphorical sense, say that the geological structure of our globe conserves the memory of all earlier cosmic changes, and that a man's body is the sedimentation of his ancestors' and his own destinies and vicissitudes. But memory is something entirely different from the fact of the structural unity and continuity of cosmic evolution. It is a phenomenon of consciousness and as such conditioned by the logical a priori. Psychologists have been puzzled by the fact that man does not remember anything from the time of his existence as an embryo and as a suckling. Freud tried to explain this absence of recollection as brought about by suppression of undesired reminiscences. The truth is that there is nothing to be remembered of unconscious states. Animal automatism and unconscious response to physiological stimulations are neither for embryos and sucklings nor for adults material for remembrance. Only conscious states can be remembered.

The human mind is not a tabula rasa on which the external events write their own history. It is equipped with a set of tools for grasping reality. Man acquires these tools, i.e., the logical structure of his mind, in the course of his evolution from an amoeba to his present state. But these tools are logically prior to any experience.

Man is not only an animal totally subject to the stimuli unavoidably determining the circumstances of his life. He is also an acting being. And the category of action is logically antecedent to any concrete act.

The fact that man does not have the creative power to imagine categories at variance with the fundamental logical relations and with the principles of causality and teleology enjoins upon us what may be called *methodological apriorism.*

Everybody in his daily behavior again and again bears witness to the immutability and universality of the categories of thought and action. He who addresses fellow men, who wants to inform and convince them, who asks questions and answers other people's questions, can proceed in this way only because he can appeal to something common to all men—namely, the logical structure of human reason. The idea that A could at the same time be *non-A* or that to prefer A to B could at the same time be to prefer B to A is simply inconceivable and absurd to a human mind. We are not in the position to comprehend any kind of prelogical or metalogical thinking. We cannot think of a world without causality and teleology.

It does not matter for man whether or not beyond the sphere accessible to the human mind there are other spheres in which there is something categorially different from human thinking and acting. No knowledge from such spheres penetrates to the human mind. It is idle to ask whether things-in-themselves are different from what they appear to us, and whether there are worlds which we cannot divine and ideas which we cannot comprehend. These are problems beyond the scope of human cognition. Human knowledge is conditioned by the structure of the human mind. If it chooses human action as the subject matter of its inquiries, it cannot mean anything else than the categories of action which are proper to the human mind and are its projection into the external world of becoming and change. All the theorems of praxeology refer only to these categories of action and are valid only in the orbit of their operation. They do not pretend to convey any information about never dreamed of and unimaginable worlds and relations.

Thus praxeology is human in a double sense. It is human because it claims for its theorems, within the sphere precisely defined in the underlying assumptions, universal validity for all human action. It is human moreover because it deals only with human action and does not aspire to know anything about nonhuman—whether subhuman or superhuman—action. . . .

The A Priori and Reality

Aprioristic reasoning is purely conceptual and deductive. It cannot produce anything else but tautologies and analytic judgments. All its implications are logically derived from the premises and were already contained in them. Hence, according to a popular objection, it cannot add anything to our knowledge.

All geometrical theorems are already implied in the axioms. The concept of a rectangular triangle already implies the theorem of Pythagoras. This theorem is a tautology, its deduction results in an analytic judgment. Nonetheless nobody would contend that geometry in general and the theorem of Pythagoras in particular do not enlarge our knowledge. Cognition from purely deductive reasoning is also creative and opens for our mind access to previously barred spheres. The significant task of aprioristic reasoning is on the one hand to bring into relief all that is implied in the categories, concepts, and premises and, on the other hand, to show what they do not imply. It is its vocation to render manifest and obvious what was hidden and unknown before.[2]

In the concept of money all the theorems of monetary theory are already implied. The quantity theory does not add to our knowledge anything which is not virtually contained in the concept of money. It transforms, develops, and unfolds; it only analyzes and is therefore tautological like the theorem of Pythagoras in relation to the concept of the rectangular triangle. However, nobody would deny the cognitive value of the quantity theory. To a mind not enlightened by economic reasoning it remains unknown. A long line of abortive attempts to solve the problems concerned shows that it was certainly not easy to attain the present state of knowledge.

It is not a deficiency of the system of aprioristic science that it does

---

[2] Science, says Meyerson, is "l'acte per lequel nous ramenons à l'identique ce qui nous a, tout d'abord, paru n'être pas tel" [the process by which we are led back to the very thing which, at first, did not seem to us to be so]. (*De l'Explication dans les sciences* [Paris, 1927], p. 154). Cf. also Morris R. Cohen, *A Preface to Logic* (New York, 1944), pp. 11–14.

not convey to us full cognition of reality. Its concepts and theorems are mental tools opening the approach to a complete grasp of reality; they are, to be sure, not in themselves already the totality of factual knowledge about all things. Theory and the comprehension of living and changing reality are not in opposition to one another. Without theory, the general aprioristic science of human action, there is no comprehension of the reality of human action.

The relation between reason and experience has long been one of the fundamental philosophical problems. Like all other problems of the critique of knowledge, philosophers have approached it only with reference to the natural sciences. They have ignored the sciences of human action. Their contributions have been useless for praxeology.

It is customary in the treatment of the epistemological problems of economics to adopt one of the solutions suggested for the natural sciences. Some authors recommend Poincaré's conventionalism.[3] Others prefer to acquiesce in ideas advanced by Einstein. Einstein raises the question: "How can mathematics, a product of human reason that does not depend on any experience, so exquisitely fit the objects of reality? Is human reason able to discover, unaided by experience through pure reasoning the features of real things?" And his answer is: "As far as the theorems of mathematics refer to reality, they are not certain, and as far as they are certain, they do not refer to reality."[4]

However, the sciences of human action differ radically from the natural sciences. All authors eager to construct an epistemological system of the sciences of human action according to the pattern of the natural sciences err lamentably.

The real thing which is the subject matter of praxeology, human action, stems from the same source as human reasoning. Action and reason are congeneric and homogeneous; they may even be called two different aspects of the same thing. That reason has the power to make clear through pure ratiocination the essential features of action is a consequence of the fact that action is an offshoot of reason. The theorems attained by correct praxeological reasoning are not only perfectly certain and incontestable, like the correct mathematical theorems. They refer, moreover, with the full rigidity of their apodictic certainty and incontestability to the reality of action as it appears in life and history. Praxeology conveys exact and precise knowledge of real things.

The starting point of praxeology is not a choice of axioms and a decision about methods of procedure, but reflection about the essence

---

[3] Henri Poincaré, *La Science et l'hypotèse* (Paris, 1918), p. 69.
[4] Felix Kaufmann, *Methodology of the Social Sciences* (London, 1944), pp. 46–47.

of action. There is no action in which the praxeological categories do not appear fully and perfectly. There is no mode of action thinkable in which means and ends or costs and proceeds cannot be clearly distinguished and precisely separated. There is nothing which only approximately or incompletely fits the economic category of an exchange. There are only exchange and nonexchange; and with regard to any exchange all the general theorems concerning exchanges are valid in their full rigidity and with all their implications. There are no transitions from exchange to nonexchange or from direct exchange to indirect exchange. No experience can ever be had which would contradict these statements.

Such an experience would be impossible in the first place for the reason that all experience concerning human action is conditioned by the praxeological categories and becomes possible only through their application. If we had not in our mind the schemes provided by praxeological reasoning, we should never be in a position to discern and to grasp any action. We would perceive motions, but neither buying nor selling, nor prices, wage rates, interest rates, and so on. It is only through the utilization of the praxeological scheme that we become able to have an experience concerning an act of buying and selling, but then independently of the fact of whether or not our senses concomitantly perceive any motions of men and of nonhuman elements of the external world. Unaided by praxeological knowledge we would never learn anything about media of exchange. If we approach coins without such preexisting knowledge, we would see in them only round plates of metal, nothing more. Experience concerning money requires familiarity with the praxeological category *medium of exchange.*

Experience concerning human action differs from that concerning natural phenomena in that it requires and presupposes praxeological knowledge. This is why the methods of the natural sciences are inappropriate for the study of praxeology, economics, and history.

In asserting the a priori character of praxeology we are not drafting a plan for a future new science different from the traditional sciences of human action. We do not maintain that the theoretical science of human action should be aprioristic, but that it is and always has been so. Every attempt to reflect upon the problems raised by human action is necessarily bound to aprioristic reasoning. It does not make any difference in this regard whether the men discussing a problem are theorists aiming at pure knowledge only or statesmen, politicians, and regular citizens eager to comprehend occurring changes and to discover what kind of public policy or private conduct would best suit their own interests. People may begin arguing about the significance of any concrete experience, but the debate inevitably turns away from the accidental and environmental features of the event concerned to an analysis of fundamental principles, and imperceptibly abandons any reference to the factual happenings which evoked the argument. The history of the natural sciences is a record of theories and hypotheses discarded because they were disproved by experience. Remember for instance the fallacies of older mechanics disproved by Galileo or the fate of the phlogiston theory. No such case is recorded by the history of economics. The champions of logically incompatible theories claim the same events as the proof that their point of view has been tested by experience. The truth is that the experience of a complex phenomenon—and there is no other experience in the realm of human action—can always be interpreted on the ground of various antithetic theories. Whether the interpretation is considered satisfactory or unsatisfactory depends on the appreciation of the theories in question established beforehand on the ground of aprioristic reasoning.[5]

History cannot teach us any general rule, principle, or law. There is no means to abstract from a historical experience a posteriori any theories or theorems concerning human conduct and policies. The data of history would be nothing but a clumsy accumulation of disconnected occurrences, a heap of confusion, if they could not be clarified, arranged, and interpreted by systematic praxeological knowledge.

The Principle of Methodological Individualism

Praxeology deals with the actions of individual men. It is only in the further course of its inquiries that cognition of human cooperation is attained and social action is treated as a special case of the more universal category of human action as such.

This methodological individualism has been vehemently attacked by various metaphysical schools and disparaged as a nominalistic fallacy. The notion of an individual, say the critics, is an empty abstraction. Real man is necessarily always a member of a social whole. It is even impossible to imagine the existence of a man separated from the rest of mankind and not connected with society. Man as man is the product of a social evolution. His most eminent feature, reason, could only emerge within the framework of social mutuality. There is no thinking which does not depend on the concepts and notions of language. But speech is manifestly a social phenomenon. Man is always the member of a collective. As the whole is both logically and tempo-

---

[5] *Cf.* E. P. Cheyney, *Law in History and Other Essays* (New York, 1927), p. 27.

rally prior to its parts or members, the study of the individual is posterior to the study of society. The only adequate method for the scientific treatment of human problems is the method of universalism or collectivism.

Now the controversy whether the whole or its parts are logically prior is vain. Logically the notions of a whole and its parts are correlative. As logical concepts they are both apart from time.

No less inappropriate with regard to our problem is the reference to the antagonism of realism and nominalism, both these terms being understood in the meaning which medieval scholasticism attached to them. It is uncontested that in the sphere of human action social entities have real existence. Nobody ventures to deny that nations, states, municipalities, parties, religious communities, are real factors determining the course of human events. Methodological individualism, far from contesting the significance of such collective wholes, considers it as one of its main tasks to describe and to analyze their becoming and their disappearing, their changing structures, and their operation. And it chooses the only method fitted to solve this problem satisfactorily.

First we must realize that all actions are performed by individuals. A collective operates always through the intermediary of one or several individuals whose actions are related to the collective as the secondary source. It is the meaning which the acting individuals and all those who are touched by their action attribute to an action, that determines its character. It is the meaning that marks one action of the state or of the municipality. The hangman, not the state, executes a criminal. It is the meaning of those concerned that discerns in the hangman's action an action of the state. A group of armed men occupies a place. It is the meaning of those concerned which imputes this occupation not to the officers and soldiers on the spot, but to their nation. If we scrutinize the meaning of the various actions performed by individuals we must necessarily learn everything about the actions of collective wholes. For a social collective has no existence and reality outside of the individual members' actions. The life of a collective is lived in the actions of the individuals constituting its body. There is no social collective conceivable which is not operative in the actions of some individuals. The reality of a social integer consists in its directing and releasing definite actions on the part of individuals. Thus the way to a cognition of collective wholes is through an analysis of the individuals' actions.

As a thinking and acting being, man emerges from his prehuman existence already as a social being. The evolution of reason, language, and cooperation is the outcome of the same process; they were inseparably and necessarily linked together. But this process took place in individuals. It consisted in changes in the behavior of individuals. There is no other substance in which it occurred than the individuals. There is no substratum of society other than the actions of individuals.

That there are nations, states, and churches, that there is social cooperation under the division of labor, becomes discernible only in the actions of certain individuals. Nobody ever perceived a nation without perceiving its members. In this sense one may say that a social collective comes into being through the actions of individuals. That does not mean that the individual is temporally antecedent. It merely means that definite actions of individuals constitute the collective.

There is no need to argue whether a collective is the sum resulting from the addition of its elements or more, whether it is a being *sui generis,* and whether it is reasonable or not to speak of its will, plans, aims, and actions and to attribute to it a distinct "soul." Such pedantic talk is idle. A collective whole is a particular aspect of the actions of various individuals and as such a real thing determining the course of events.

It is illusory to believe that it is possible to visualize collective wholes. They are never visible; their cognition is always the outcome of the understanding of the meaning which acting men attribute to their acts. We can see a crowd, i.e., a multitude of people. Whether this crowd is a mere gathering or a mass (in the sense in which this term is used in contemporary psychology) or an organized body or any other kind of social entity is a question which can only be answered by understanding the meaning which they themselves attach to their presence. And this meaning is always the meaning of individuals. Not our senses, but understanding, a mental process, makes us recognize social entities.

Those who want to start the study of human action from the collective units encounter an insurmountable obstacle in the fact that an individual at the same time can belong and—with the exception of the most primitive tribesmen—really belongs to various collective entities. The problems raised by the multiplicity of coexisting social units and their mutual antagonisms can be solved only by methodological individualism.

I and We

The *Ego* is the unity of the acting being. It is unquestionably given and cannot be dissolved or conjured away by any reasoning or quibbling.

The *We* is always the result of a summing up which puts together two or more *Egos.* If somebody says, *I,* no further question is necessary in order to establish the meaning. The same is valid with regard to the *Thou* and, provided the person in view is precisely indicated, with regard to the *He.* But if a man says *We,* further information is needed to denote who the Egos are who are comprised in this *We.* It is always single individuals who say *We;* even if they say it in chorus, it yet remains an utterance of single individuals.

The *We* cannot act otherwise than each of them acting on his own behalf. They can either all act together in accord, or one of them may act for them all. In the latter case the cooperation of the others consists in their bringing about the situation which makes one man's action effective for them too. Only in this sense does the officer of a social entity act for the whole; the individual members of the collective body either cause or allow a single man's action to concern them too.

The endeavors of psychology to dissolve the *Ego* and to unmask it as an illusion are idle. The praxeological *Ego* is beyond any doubts. No matter what a man was and what he may become later, in the very act of choosing and acting he is an *Ego.*

From the *pluralis logicus* (and from the merely ceremonial *pluralis majestaticus*) we must distinguish the *pluralis gloriosus.* If a Canadian who never tried skating says, "We are the world's foremost ice hockey players," or if an Italian boor proudly contends, "We are the world's most eminent painters," nobody is fooled. But with reference to political and economic problems the *pluralis gloriosus* evolves into the *pluralis imperialis* and as such plays a significant role in paving the way for the acceptance of doctrines determining international economic policies.

The Principle of Methodological Singularism

No less than from the action of an individual, praxeology begins its investigations from the individual action. It does not deal in vague terms with human action in general, but with concrete action which a definite man has performed at a definite date and at a definite place. But, of course, it does not concern itself with the accidental and environmental features of this action and with what distinguishes it from all other actions, but only with what is necessary and universal in its performance.

The philosophy of universalism [collectivism] has from time immemorial blocked access to a satisfactory grasp of praxeological problems, and contemporary universalists are utterly incapable of finding an approach to them. Universalism, collectivism, and conceptual realism see only wholes and universals. They speculate about mankind, nations, states, classes, about virtue and vice, right and wrong, about entire classes of wants and of commodities. They ask, for instance: Why is the value of "gold" higher than that of "iron"? Thus they never find solutions, but antinomies and paradoxes only. The best known instance is the value-paradox which frustrated even the work of Classical economists.

Praxeology asks: What happens in acting? What does it mean to say that an individual then and there, today and here, at any time and at any place, acts? What results if he chooses one thing and rejects another?

The act of choosing is always a decision among various opportunities open to the choosing individual. Man never chooses between virtue and vice, but only between two modes of action which we call from an adopted point of view virtuous or vicious. A man never chooses between "gold" and "iron" in general, but always only between a definite quantity of gold and a definite quantity of iron. Every single action is strictly limited in its immediate consequences. If we want to reach correct conclusions, we must first of all look at these limitations.

Human life is an unceasing sequence of single actions. But the single action is by no means isolated. It is a link in a chain of actions which together form an action on a higher level aiming at a more distant end. Every action has two aspects. It is on the one hand a partial action in the framework of a further-stretching action, the performance of a fraction of the aims set by a more far-reaching action. It is on the other hand itself a whole with regard to the actions aimed at by the performance of its own parts.

It depends upon the scope of the project on which acting man is intent at the instant whether the more far-reaching action or a partial action directed to a more immediate end only is thrown into relief. There is no need for praxeology to raise questions of the type of those raised by *Gestaltpsychologie*. The road to the performance of great things must always lead through the performance of partial tasks. A cathedral is something other than a heap of stones joined together. But the only procedure for constructing a cathedral is to lay one stone upon another. For the architect the whole project is the main thing. For the mason it is the single wall, and for the bricklayer the single stones. What counts for praxeology is the fact that the only method to achieve greater tasks is to build from the foundations step by step, part by part.

The Individual and Changing Features of Human Action

The content of human action, i.e., the ends aimed at and the means chosen and applied for the attainment of these ends, is determined by the personal qualities of every acting man. Individual man is the product of a long line of zoological evolution which has shaped his physiological inheritance. He is born the offspring and the heir of his ancestors, and the precipitate and sediment of all that his forefathers experienced are his biological patrimony. When he is born, he does not enter the world in general as such, but a definite environment. The innate and inherited biological qualities and all that life has worked upon him make a man what he is at any instant of his pilgrimage. They are his fate and destiny. His will is not "free" in the metaphysical sense of this term. It is determined by his background and all the influences to which he himself and his ancestors were exposed.

Inheritance and environment direct a man's actions. They suggest to him both the ends and the means. He lives not simply as man *in abstracto;* he lives as a son of his family, his race, his people, and his age; as a citizen of his country; as a member of a definite social group; as a practitioner of a certain vocation; as a follower of definite religious, metaphysical, philosophical, and political ideas; as a partisan in many feuds and controversies. He does not himself create his ideas and standards of value; he borrows them from other people. His ideology is what his environment enjoins upon him. Only very few men have the gift of thinking new and original ideas and of changing the traditional body of creeds and doctrines.

Common man does not speculate about the great problems. With regard to them he relies upon other people's authority, he behaves as "every decent fellow must behave," he is like a sheep in the herd. It is precisely this intellectual inertia that characterizes a man as a common man. Yet the common man does choose. He chooses to adopt traditional patterns or patterns adopted by other people because he is convinced that this procedure is best fitted to achieve his own welfare. And he is ready to change his ideology and consequently his mode of action whenever he becomes convinced that this would better serve his own interests.

Most of a man's daily behavior is simple routine. He performs certain acts without paying special attention to them. He does many things because he was trained in his childhood to do them, because other people behave in the same way, and because it is customary in his environment. He acquires habits, he develops automatic reactions. But he indulges in these habits only because he welcomes their effects. As soon as he discovers that the pursuit of the habitual way may hinder the attainment of ends considered as more desirable, he changes his attitude. A man brought up in an area in which the water is clean acquires the habit of heedlessly drinking, washing, and bathing. When he moves to a place in which the water is polluted by morbific germs, he will devote the most careful attention to procedures about which he never bothered before. He will watch himself permanently in order not to hurt himself by indulging unthinkingly in his traditional routine and his automatic reactions. The fact that an action is in the regular course of affairs performed spontaneously, as it were, does not mean that it is not due to a conscious volition and to a deliberate choice. Indulgence in a routine which possibly could be changed is action.

Praxeology is not concerned with the changing content of acting, but with its pure form and its categorical structure. The study of the accidental and environmental features of human action is the task of history. . . .

History deals with unique and unrepeatable events, with the irreversible flux of human affairs. A historical event cannot be described without reference to the persons involved and to the place and date of its occurrence. As far as a happening can be narrated without such a reference, it is not a historical event but a fact of the natural sciences. The report that Professor X on February 20, 1945, performed a certain experiment in his laboratory is an account of a historical event. The physicist believes that he is right in abstracting from the person of the experimenter and the date and place of the experiment. He relates only those circumstances which, in his opinion, are relevant for the production of the result achieved and, when repeated, will produce the same result again. He transforms the historical event into *a fact* of the empirical natural sciences. He disregards the active interference of the experimenter and tries to imagine him as an indifferent observer and relater of unadulterated reality. It is not the task of praxeology to deal with the epistemological issues of this philosophy.

Although unique and unrepeatable, historical events have one common feature: they are human action. History comprehends them as human actions; it conceives their meaning by the instrumentality of praxeological cognition and understands their meaning in looking at their individual and unique features. What counts for history is always the meaning of the men concerned: the meaning that they attach to the state of affairs they want to alter, the meaning they attach to their actions, and the meaning they attach to the effects produced by the actions. . . .

It was a fundamental mistake of the Historical school of *Wirtschaftliche Staatswissenschaften* in Germany and of Institutionalism in America to interpret economics as the characterization of the behavior of an ideal type, the *homo oeconomicus*. According to this doctrine traditional or orthodox economics does not deal with the behavior of man as he really is and acts, but with a fictitious or hypothetical image. It pictures a being driven exclusively by "economic" motives, i.e., solely by the intention of making the greatest possible material or monetary profit. Such a being, say these critics, does not have and never did have a counterpart in reality; it is a phantom of a spurious armchair philosophy. No man is exclusively motivated by the desire to become as rich as possible; many are not at all influenced by this mean craving. It is vain to refer to such an illusory homunculus in dealing with life and history. . . .

The Classical economists sought to explain the formation of prices. They were fully aware of the fact that prices are not a product of the activities of a special group of people, but the result of an interplay of all members of the market society. This was the meaning of their statement that demand and supply determine the formation of prices. However, the Classical economists failed in their endeavors to provide a satisfactory theory of value. They were at a loss to find a solution for the apparent paradox of value. They were puzzled by the alleged paradox that "gold" is more highly valued than "iron," although the latter is more "useful" than the former. Thus they could not construct a general theory of value and could not trace back the phenomena of market exchange and of production to their ultimate sources, the behavior of the consumers. This shortcoming forced them to abandon their ambitious plan to develop a general theory of human action. They had to satisfy themselves with a theory explaining only the activities of the businessman without going back to the choices of everybody as the ultimate determinants. They dealt only with the actions of businessmen eager to buy in the cheapest market and to sell in the dearest. The consumer was left outside the field of their theorizing. Later the epigones of Classical economics explained and justified this insufficiency as an intentional and methodologically necessary procedure. It was, they asserted, the deliberate design of economists to restrict their investigations to only one aspect of human endeavor—namely, to the "economic" aspect. It was their intention to use the fictitious image of a man driven solely by "economic" motives and to neglect all others although they were fully aware of the fact that real men are driven by many other, "noneconomic" motives. To deal with these other motives, one group of these interpreters maintained, is not the task of economics but of other branches of knowledge. Another group admitted that the treatment of these "noneconomic" motives and their influence on the formation of prices was a task of economics also, but they believed that it must be left to later generations. It will be shown at a later stage of our investigations that this distinction between "economic" and "noneconomic" motives of human action is untenable.* At this point it is only important to realize that this doctrine of the "economic" side of human action utterly misrepresents the teachings of the Classical economists. They never intended to do what this doctrine ascribes to them. They wanted to conceive the real formation of prices—not fictitious prices as they would be determined if men were acting under the sway of hypothetical conditions different from those really influencing them. The prices they try to explain and do explain—although without tracing them back to the choices of the consumers—are real market prices. The demand and supply of which they speak are real factors determined by all motives instigating men to buy or to sell. What was wrong with their theory was that they did not trace demand back to the choices of the consumers; they lacked a satisfactory theory of demand. But it was not their idea that demand as they used this concept in their dissertations was exclusively determined by "economic" motives as distinguished from "noneconomic" motives. As they restricted their theorizing to the actions of businessmen, they did not deal with the motives of the ultimate consumers. Nonetheless their theory of prices was intended as an explanation of real prices irrespective of the motives and ideas instigating the consumers.

Modern subjective economics starts with the solution of the apparent paradox of value. It neither limits its theorems to the actions of businessmen alone nor deals with a fictitious *homo oeconomicus.* It treats the inexorable categories of everybody's action. Its theorems concerning commodity prices, wage rates, and interest rates refer to all these phenomena without any regard to the motives causing people to buy or to sell or to abstain from buying or selling. It is time to discard entirely any reference to the abortive attempt to justify the shortcoming of older economists through the appeal to the *homo oeconomicus* phantom.

---

*Editor's note: See *Human Action,* 3rd (1966) or 4th (1996) ed., pp. 232–234, 239–243, 882–885. Also above, pp. 119–122, 129.

The Procedure of Economics

The scope of praxeology is the explication of the category of human action. All that is needed for the deduction of all praxeological theorems is knowledge of the essence of human action. It is a knowledge that is our own because we are men; no being of human descent that pathological conditions have not reduced to a merely vegetative existence lacks it. No special experience is needed in order to comprehend these theorems, and no experience, however rich, could disclose them to a being who did not know a priori what human action is. The only way to a cognition of these theorems is logical analysis of our inherent knowledge of the category of action. We must bethink ourselves and reflect upon the structure of human action. Like logic and mathematics, praxeological knowledge is in us; it does not come from without.

All the concepts and theorems of praxeology are implied in the category of human action. The first task is to extract and to deduce them, to expound their implications and to define the universal conditions of acting as such. Having shown what conditions are required by any action, one must go further and define—of course, in a categorial and formal sense—the less general conditions required for special modes of acting. It would be possible to deal with this second task by delineating all thinkable conditions and deducing from them all inferences logically permissible. Such an all-comprehensive system would provide a theory referring not only to human action as it is under the conditions and circumstances given in the real world in which man lives and acts. It would deal no less with hypothetical acting such as would take place under the unrealizable conditions of imaginary worlds.

But the end of science is to know reality. It is not mental gymnastics or a logical pastime. Therefore praxeology restricts its inquiries to the study of acting under those conditions and presuppositions which are given in reality. It studies acting under unrealized and unrealizable conditions only from two points of view. It deals with states of affairs which, although not real in the present and past world, could possibly become real at some future date. And it examines unreal and unrealizable conditions if such an inquiry is needed for a satisfactory grasp of what is going on under the conditions present in reality.

However, this reference to experience does not impair the aprioristic character of praxeology and economics. Experience merely directs our curiosity toward certain problems and diverts it from other problems. It tells us what we should explore, but it does not tell us how we could proceed in our search for knowledge. Moreover, it is not experience but thinking alone which teaches us that, and in what instances, it is necessary to investigate unrealizable hypothetical conditions in order to conceive what is going on in the real world.

The disutility of labor is not of a categorial and aprioristic character. We can without contradiction think of a world in which labor does not cause uneasiness, and we can depict the state of affairs prevailing in such a world.[6] But the real world is conditioned by the disutility of labor. Only theorems based on the assumption that labor is a source of uneasiness are applicable for the comprehension of what is going on in this world.

Experience teaches that there is disutility of labor. But it does not teach it directly. There is no phenomenon that introduces itself as disutility of labor. There are only data of experience which are interpreted, on the ground of aprioristic knowledge, to mean that men consider leisure—i.e., the absence of labor—other things being equal, as a more desirable condition than the expenditure of labor. We see that men renounce advantages which they could get by working more—that is, that they are ready to make sacrifices for the attainment of leisure. We infer from this fact that leisure is valued as a good and that labor is regarded as a burden. But for previous praxeological insight, we would never be in a position to reach this conclusion.

A theory of indirect exchange and all further theories built upon it—as the theory of circulation credit— are applicable only to the interpretation of events within a world in which indirect exchange is practiced. In a world of barter trade only it would be mere intellectual play. It is unlikely that the economists of such a world, if economic science could have emerged at all in it, would have given any thought to the problems of indirect exchange, money, and all the rest. In our actual world, however, such studies are an essential part of economic theory.

The fact that praxeology, in fixing its eye on the comprehension of reality, concentrates upon the investigation of those problems which are useful for this purpose, does not alter the aprioristic character of its reasoning. But it marks the way in which economics, up to now the only elaborated part of praxeology, presents the results of its endeavors.

Economics does not follow the procedure of logic and mathematics. It does not present an integrated system of pure aprioristic ratiocination severed from any reference to reality. In introducing assumptions into its reasoning, it satisfies itself that the treatment of the assumptions concerned can render useful services for the comprehension of reality. It does not strictly separate in its treatises and mono-

---

[6] See Mises' *Human Action*, 3rd ed., 1966; 4th ed., 1996, pp. 131–133.

graphs pure science from the application of its theorems to the solution of concrete historical and political problems. It adopts for the organized presentation of its results a form in which aprioristic theory and the interpretation of historical phenomena are intertwined.

It is obvious that this mode of procedure is enjoined upon economics by the very nature and essence of its subject matter. It has given proof of its expediency. However, one must not overlook the fact that the manipulation of this singular and logically somewhat strange procedure requires caution and subtlety, and that uncritical and superficial minds have again and again been led astray by careless confusion of the two epistemologically different methods implied.

There are no such things as a historical method of economics or a discipline of institutional economics. There is economics and there is economic history. The two must never be confused. All theorems of economics are necessarily valid in every instance in which all the assumptions presupposed are given. Of course, they have no practical significance in situations where these conditions are not present. The theorems referring to indirect exchange are not applicable to conditions where there is no indirect exchange. But this does not impair their validity.[7]

The issue has been obfuscated by the endeavors of government and powerful pressure groups to disparage economics and to defame the economists. Despots and democratic majorities are drunk with power. They must reluctantly admit that they are subject to the laws of nature. But they reject the very notion of economic law. Are they not the supreme legislators? Don't they have the power to crush every opponent? No war lord is prone to acknowledge any limits other than those imposed on him by a superior armed force. Servile scribblers are always ready to foster such complacency by expounding the appropriate doctrines. They call their garbled presumptions "historical economics." In fact, economic history is a long record of government policies that failed because they were designed with a bold disregard for the laws of economics.

It is impossible to understand the history of economic thought if one does not pay attention to the fact that economics as such is a challenge to the conceit of those in power. An economist can never be a favorite of autocrats and demagogues. With them he is always the mischief-maker, and the more they are inwardly convinced that his objections are well founded, the more they hate him.

In the face of all this frenzied agitation it is expedient to establish

---

[7] Cf. F. H. Knight, *The Ethics of Competition and Other Essays* (New York, 1935), p. 139.

the fact that the starting point of all praxeological and economic reasoning, the category of human action, is proof against any criticisms and objections. No appeal to any historical or empirical considerations whatever can discover any fault in the proposition that men purposefully aim at certain chosen ends. No talk about irrationality, the unfathomable depths of the human soul, the spontaneity of the phenomena of life, automatisms, reflexes, and tropisms, can invalidate the statement that man makes use of his reason for the realization of wishes and desires. From the unshakable foundation of the category of human action praxeology and economics proceed step by step by means of discursive reasoning. Precisely defining assumptions and conditions, they construct a system of concepts and draw all the inferences implied by logically unassailable ratiocination. With regard to the results thus obtained only two attitudes are possible: either one can unmask logical errors in the chain of the deductions which produced these results, or one must acknowledge their correctness and validity.

It is vain to object that life and reality are not logical. Life and reality are neither logical nor illogical; they are simply given. But logic is the only tool available to man for the comprehension of both. It is vain to object that life and history are inscrutable and ineffable and that human reason can never penetrate to their inner core. The critics contradict themselves in uttering words about the ineffable and expanding theories—of course, spurious theories—about the unfathomable. There are many things beyond the reach of the human mind. But as far as man is able to attain any knowledge, however limited, he can use only one avenue of approach, that opened by reason.

No less illusory are the endeavors to play off understanding against the theorems of economics. The domain of historical understanding is exclusively the elucidation of those problems which cannot be entirely elucidated by the nonhistorical sciences. Understanding must never contradict the theories developed by the nonhistorical sciences. Understanding can never do anything but, on the one hand, establish the fact that people were motivated by certain ideas, aimed at certain ends, and applied certain means for the attainment of these ends, and, on the other hand, assign to the various historical factors their relevance so far as this cannot be achieved by the nonhistorical sciences. Understanding does not entitle the modern historian to assert that exorcism ever was an appropriate means to cure sick cows. Neither does it permit him to maintain that an economic law was not valid in ancient Rome or in the empire of the Incas.

Man is not infallible. He searches for truth—that is, for the most adequate comprehension of reality as far as the structure of his mind and reason makes it accessible to him. Man can never become omniscient. He can never be absolutely certain that his inquiries were not misled and that what he considers as certain truth is not error. All that man can do is to submit all his theories again and again to the most critical reexamination. This means for the economist to trace back all theorems to their unquestionable and certain ultimate basis, the category of human action, and to test by the most careful scrutiny all assumptions and inferences leading from this basis to the theorem under examination. It cannot be contended that this procedure is a guarantee against error. But it is undoubtedly the most effective method of avoiding error.

Praxeology—and consequently economics too—is a deductive system. It draws its strength from the starting point of its deductions, from the category of action. No economic theorem can be considered sound that is not solidly fastened upon this foundation by an irrefutable chain of reasoning. A statement proclaimed without such a connection is arbitrary and floats in midair. It is impossible to deal with a special segment of economics if one does not encase it in a complete system of action.

The empirical sciences start from singular events and proceed from the unique and individual to the more universal. Their treatment is subject to specialization. They can deal with segments without paying attention to the whole field. The economist must never be a specialist. In dealing with any problem he must always fix his glance upon the whole system.

References for Further Study

Böhm-Bawerk, Eugen von. *Capital and Interest.* 3 vols. Translated from the German (1889/1902/1921) by George D. Huncke, Hans F. Sennholz, consulting economist. With a Preface by Hans F. Sennholz. South Holland, Ill.: Libertarian Press, 1959. I, xxii: 490; II, xi: 466; III, viii: 246.

———. *Value and Price.* Extract from *Capital and Interest* (Volume II, Book III) published separately. South Holland, Ill.: Libertarian Press, 1960, 1973.

Caldwell, Bruce J., ed. *Carl Menger and his Legacy in Economics.* Durham, N.C.: Duke University Press, 1990, 407 pp. See especially Israel Kirzner's "Menger, Classical Liberalism, and the Austrian School of Economics," Karl Milford's "Menger's Methodology," and Karen I. Vaughn's "The Mengerian Roots of the Austrian Revival."

Cubbedu, Raimondo. *The Philosophy of the Austrian School.* Translated by Rachel M. Costa, née Barritt. London & New York: Routledge, 1993. 254 pp.

Dolan, Edwin G., ed. *The Foundations of Modern Austrian Economics.* Kansas City: Sheed & Ward, Inc., 1976. ix: 238 pp.

Ebeling, Richard M., ed. *Austrian Economics: A Reader.* The Ludwig von Mises Lecture Series, Vol. 18. Hillsdale, Mich.: Hillsdale College Press, 1991. 692 pp. See especially essays in Part II, "Philosophy and Method of the Austrian School."

Greaves, Percy L., Jr. *Mises Made Easier: A Glossary for Ludwig von Mises' HUMAN ACTION.* Irvington, N.Y.: Free Market Books, 1990. xviii: 158 pp. (1st ed., Dobbs Ferry, N.Y.: Free Market Books, 1974).

———. *Understanding the Dollar Crisis.* Dobbs Ferry, N.Y.: Free Market Books, 1984. xxiv: 308 pp. (1st ed., Belmont, Mass.: Western Islands, 1973).

Hayek, F. A. "Economic Thought: The Austrian School." *International Encyclopedia of the Social Sciences.* 4: 458–462. London: Macmillan; New York: The Free Press, 1968. Reprinted as "The Austrian School of Economics" in *The Collected Works of F. A. Hayek: IV. The Fortunes of Liberalism.* Peter G. Klein, ed. Chicago: University of Chicago Press, 1992, pp. 42–60.

Hazlitt, Henry. *The Failure of the "New Economics."* New edition with introduction by Hans F. Sennholz. Irvington-on-Hudson, N.Y.:

Foundation for Economic Education, 1994. xiv 458 pp. (1st ed., Princeton, N.J.: D. Van Nostrand, 1959; 2nd ed. New Rochelle, N.Y.: Arlington House, 1977).

———. *The Foundations of Morality.* Hazlitt Centennial edition. Irvington-on-Hudson, N.Y.: Foundation for Economic Education, 1994. xvi: 398 pp. (1st ed., Princeton, N.J.: D. Van Nostrand, 1964; 2nd ed., Los Angeles: Nash Publishing, 1972).

Herbener, Jeffrey M., ed. *The Meaning of Ludwig von Mises.* Studies in Austrian Economics Series. Auburn, Ala.: Praxeology Press of the Ludwig von Mises Institute; Kluwer Academic Publishers, 1993. 350 pp.

Hoppe, Hans-Hermann. *Economic Science and the Austrian Method.* Auburn, Ala.: Ludwig von Mises Institute, 1995. 88 pp.

Kauder, Emil. *A History of Marginal Utility Theory.* Princeton, N.J.: Princeton University Press, 1965. xxii: 248 pp.

Kirzner, Israel M. "Austrian School of Economics." *The New Palgrave: A Dictionary of Economics.* London: Macmillan; New York: Stockton Press, 1987. 1:145–151.

———, ed. *Classics in Austrian Economics: A Sampling in the History of a Tradition.* 3 vols. London: William Pickering, 1994. Vol. I. The Founding Era, xxxii: 355 pp. Vol. II. The Interwar Period, xx: 340 pp. Vol. III. The Age of Mises and Hayek, xviii: 312 pp.

———. "Divergent Approaches in Libertarian Economic Thought." *Intercollegiate Review.* 3:3 (January- February 1967), pp. 101–108.

———. *The Economic Point of View: An Essay in the History of Economic Thought.* Kansas City: Sheed & Ward, 1976. xix:228 pp. (1st ed., Princeton, N.J.: D. Van Nostrand, 1960).

———. *The Meaning of Market Process: Essays in the Development of Modern Austrian Economics.* London/New York: Routledge, 1992. xii: 246 pp.

———. *Method, Process and Austrian Economics: Essays in Honor of Ludwig von Mises.* Lexington, Mass.: Lexington Books; D. C. Heath & Co., 1982. viii: 263 pp.

Littlechild, Stephen, ed. *Austrian Economics.* 3 vols. Aldershot, Hants, England; Brookfield, Vt.: Edgar Elgar, 1990. Vol I, xx: 538 pp. Vol. II, xvi: 386 pp. Vol. III, xx: 454 pp.

Menger, Carl. *Investigations into the Method of the Social Sciences.* Translated from the German (1883) by Francis J. Nock. Grove City, Pa.: Libertarian Press, 1996. xxii: 234 pp. (First published in English as *Problems of Economics and Sociology.* Urbana, Ill.: University of Illinois Press, 1963. Reprinted 1985 by New York University Press as

Investigations into the Method of the Social Sciences with Special Reference to Economics.)

——. *Principles of Economics.* First German edition, 1871. Translated by James Dingwall and Bert F. Hoselitz. Introduction by F. A. Hayek. Grove City, Pa.: Libertarian Press, 1994. 328 pp. (First English-language edition, Glencoe, Ill.: The Free Press, 1950; Institute for Humane Studies, New York University Press, 1976).

Mises, Ludwig von. *Epistemological Problems of Economics.* First published in German, 1933. Translated by George Reisman. New York University Press, 1981. xxxi: 239 pp. (First English-language edition, Princeton, N.J.: D. Van Nostrand, 1960).

——. *Human Action: An Economic Treatise.* 4th ed., Irvington-on-Hudson, N.Y.: Foundation for Economic Education, 1996. xix: 907 pp. (1st ed., New Haven: Yale University Press, 1949; 2nd ed., Yale University Press, 1966; 3rd ed., Chicago: Henry Regnery Co., 1966).

——. *Theory and History,* with a new Preface by Murray N. Rothbard. Auburn, Ala.: Ludwig von Mises Institute, 1985. xvi: 384 pp. (1st ed., New Haven: Yale University Press, 1957; 2nd ed., New Rochelle, N.Y.: Arlington House, 1969).

——. *The Ultimate Foundation of Economic Science: An Essay on Method* with a new Foreword by Israel M. Kirzner. Kansas City : Sheed Andrews & McMeel, 1978. xvii: 148 pp. (1st ed., Princeton, N.J.: D. Van Nostrand, 1962).

Rothbard, Murray N. "In Defense of 'Extreme Apriorism'," *Southern Economic Journal.* 23:3 (January 1957), pp. 314–320. Reprinted in *Austrian Economics I.* Stephen Littlechild, ed., pp. 445–451.

——. *The Present State of Austrian Economics: A Working Paper from the Ludwig von Mises Institute.* Auburn, Ala.: Auburn University, November 1992. 44 pp.

Selgin, George A. *Praxeology and Understanding: An Analysis of the Controversy in Austrian Economics.* Auburn, Ala.: Ludwig von Mises Institute, 1990. 74 pp.

Sennholz, Hans F. "Chicago Monetary Tradition in the Light of Austrian Theory." *Toward Liberty: Essays in Honor of Ludwig von Mises on the Occasion of his 90th Birthday, September 29, 1971.* Menlo Park, Calif.: Institute for Humane Studies, Inc., 1971, pp. 347–366. Reprinted (pp. 39–54) in Hans F. Sennholz, *Age of Inflation.* Belmont, Mass.: Western Islands, 1979. vii: 207 pp.

Sennholz, Mary, ed. *On Freedom and Free Enterprise: Essays in Honor of Ludwig von Mises, Presented on the Occasion of the Fiftieth Anniversary of his Doctorate, February 20, 1956.* Revised edition, Irvington-on-

Hudson, N.Y.: Foundation for Economic Education, 1994. xiii: 333 pp. See especially Murray N. Rothbard's "Toward a Reconstruction of Utility and Welfare Economics," pp. 224–262, and Louis M. Spadaro's "Averages and Aggregates in Economics," pp. 140–160. (1st ed., Princeton, N.J.: D. Van Nostrand, 1956).

Spangler, Mark and John Robbins, eds. *A Man of Principle: Essays in Honor of Hans F. Sennholz.* Grove City, Pa.: Grove City College Press, 1992. xvii: 571 pp. See especially Juan C. Cachanosky's "The Theory of Value and the Austrian School," pp. 75–89, Israel M. Kirzner's "Human Action, Freedom, and Economic Science," pp. 241–249, and Lawrence W. Reed's "The Perils of Forecasting," pp. 363–372.

Vaughn, Karen I. *Austrian Economics in America: The Migration of a Tradition.* New York: Cambridge University Press, 1994. 198 pp.

White, Lawrence H. *The Methodology of the Austrian School Economists.* Auburn, Ala.: Ludwig von Mises Institute, 1984. 40 pp. (1st ed., New York: Center for Libertarian Studies, 1977).

Index

Academic freedom, 55–56, 77–78
Action
 apriori axiom, 3, 120–122, 124, 141,
  142–144, 147–148, 149–150
 economic calculation and, 128–129
Althoff, Friedrich, 64
Amonn, Alfred, 73
Apriorism, methodological, 137–144,
  152–157
Aprioristic reasoning, 141–144,
  153–156
Araki, Kotari, 80
Auspitz, Rudolf, 73
Austrian economics. *See* Action; Final
  utility; Methodological individualism; Value
Austrian school of economics, 85–88,
  96–104
 government and, 69–72, 99
 historical setting, 53–82
 intellectual climate and, 57–58, 71- 72
 Menger and, 47–52, 53–54
 universities and, 54–56

Bagehot, Walter, 48–49
Bendixen, Friedrich, 52
Bentham, Jeremy, 126
Bergson, Henri, 57, 137n
Berlin, University of, 36–40
Bettelheim-Gabillon, Ludwig, 59
Bismarck, Otto von, 66
Böhm-Bawerk, Eugen von, 2, 11, 15,
  17, 21, 25, 29, 35, 44–46, 51, 54,
  56, 58–59, 74, 108, 124
 critique of, 27–28, 105, 106–107,
  108, 112–118, 123
 government and, 58–59, 70–72
 objective value, 19, 22, 27, 30
 university seminar, 44–46
Bois-Reymond, Emil du, 64

Bolzano, Bernard, 53, 55
Brentano, Lujo, 55, 67

Capital, wealth, 23, 29, 32
Cassel, Gustav, 52
Catallactics, 3, 105–106, 108, 121–122,
  133–134
Clark, John Bates, 50, 88
Classical school of economics, 1,
  47–48, 49, 60–62, 75–76, 85, 86,
  99–103, 119–120, 134–136,
  151–152
 time and, 131–133
 home oeconomicus, 116–117, 151–152
 paradox of value, 2, 14–15, 49, 106,
  112, 119, 148, 151–152
Collectives, collectivism, 125,
  144–146, 147
Compulsion, 75. *See also* Government
  intervention
Conceptual realism, 125
Cooperation, peaceful, 74–76
Cost, 23–26, 91–97, 134–136
Crusoe economy, 100
Čuhel, Franz, 74, 131

Demand. *See* Supply and demand
Diehl, Karl, 107–108
Dietzel, Heinrich, 19, 29, 67
Distribution, final utility and, 97–98

Economic, monetary, calculation,
  128–131
Economic history, 3, 131, 155
Economics
 in broader/narrower sense, 129
 procedure of, 152–157
 psychology and, 27–28, 71, 124–126
 technology and, 127
 theory and, 49, 97–100

Einstein, Albert, 142
Engliš, Karel, 74
Enlightenment, 60, 69
Epicurus, 123
Equilibrium, 131, 132–133
Ethics, 122–124
Eudaemonism, 122–124
Exchange, 89, 105–106, 119–121,
    125–126

Factors of production. *See* Goods,
    complementary
Feuerbach, Ludwig, 63
Final utility, 17–18, 24–27, 29–30,
    87–89, 102
  complementary goods and, 95–98
  cost and, 91–97
  exchange and, 89
  price and, 20–23, 26–27, 30, 90
Foundation for Economic Education,
    3
Freud, Sigmund, 53, 55, 57
Frictional resistances, 133–134
Froelich, Walter, 79

Gaitskell, Hugh, 80
Galilei, Galileo, 144
George, Henry, 127
German Historical school. *See* Histor-
    ical school
Germany
  Marxism and, 67–69
  Nazism and, 67, 68–69, 75–76, 81
Goods
  land, 127
  ranks/orders of, 23–27, 98
  complementary, 23–27, 94–98
Gossen, Hermann Heinrich, 50, 64,
    88, 124–125, 126
Government intervention, 48, 75–76,
    133–134, 155
Greaves, Bettina (Bien), 4
Greaves, Percy L., Jr., 4

Haberler, Gottfried, 79, 81
Hayek, Friedrich A., 4, 70–71, 79, 80,
    81

Hazlitt, Henry, 4
Hedonism, 123
Hermann, F. B. W. von, 64
Historical school (German), 3, 33–40,
    51–52, 56, 60–64, 85, 87, 151
  government and, 62, 63–64, 66–69,
    75–76
  methodology, 61–62, 96, 103–
    104
History, 144, 150, 155–156
Hitler, Adolf, 69
Human action, 142–144, 149–150,
    152–157
Hume, David, 70
Hutt, W. H., 4

Ideas and intellectual progress,
    70–72
Institute for Humane Studies, 4
Institutionalism, 151
Interest, time and, 25
Intervention. *See* Government inter-
    vention

Jacobi, F. H., 123–124
Jenks, Jeremiah, 80
Jevons, William Stanley, 11–12, 27,
    29–30, 50, 53, 88, 101
Jhering, Rudolf von, 55, 63

Kaufmann, Felix, 80
Keckeissen, Joseph, 4
Keynesianism, 3
Kirzner, Israel M., 4
Knies, Karl, 54, 64
Koether, George, 4
Komorzynski, Johann von, 74

Labor, wages, 29–30, 31–32
Lachmann, Ludwig M., 4
Land, 30, 127
Lauderdale, James Maitland, 29
Lexis, Wilhelm, 68
Liberal Party, Austrian, 54–56
Liberalism, 48, 69–72
Lieben, Richard, 73
Logic, 3, 138–140, 156

Mach, Ernst, positivism and the "Vienna Circle," 55
Machlup, Fritz, 78–79, 81
MacVane, Silas Marcus, 101
Mangoldt, Hans von, 64
Marginal utility, 2, 135. *See also* Final utility; Value
Marshall, Alfred, 34
Marxism, 67–68
Mayer, Hans, 74
Mendel, Gregor, 53
Menger, Carl, 2, 11–13, 15ff., 29, 34–35, 56, 70–72, 74, 98, 117
  Austrian school and, 47–52, 53–54
  capital, wealth and 23, 30
  critique of, 105, 108–111, 117–118
  government and, 59, 70–71
  methodology of, 33–35, 49, 64–65
  Methodenstreit and, 65, 86–87
  university teaching, 42–44, 46
Mercantilism, 48
Methodenstreit (struggle over methods), 3, 33–35, 49, 64–69, 74–76, 86–87
Methodological apriorism, 140
Methodological individualism, 2, 6, 7, 125, 144–147
Methodological singularism, 147
Methodology
  Austrian, 2–3, 4–5, 6–7
  economic, 133–134
  historical, empirical, 5, 6, 61–62
  Menger's, 33–35, 49, 64–65
  See also Methodological individualism; Value
Meyer, Robert, 74
Meyerson, Émile, 141n
Mill, John Stuart, 11, 28–29, 61
Mintz, Ilse, 79
Mises, Ludwig von, 3
  Institute for Business Cycle Research, 81
  Monetary or circulation credit theory of the trade cycle, 73–74, 132–133
  NYU graduate seminar, 3–4
  Privatseminar, 58, 79–81

Monetary or circulation credit theory of the trade cycle, 73–74, 132–133
Money, 128–129, 141
Mont Pèlerin Society, 4
Morgenstern, Oskar, 79, 81
Murata, Toshio, 4

New York University Graduate School of Business Administration, 3–4
Nietzsche, Friedrich Wilhelm, 75
Nominalism, 125

Oppenheimer, Franz, 127
Oswalt, Heinrich, 50, 57

Perroux, François, 80
Peterson, William H., 4
Philippovich von Philippsberg, Eugen, 41n
Physiocrats, 47
Poincaré, Henri, 142
Population, 127
Positivism, 60–61, 65, 77, 78
Praxeology, 3, 137–141, 142–144, 147–148, 152–157
Predictions, economic, 5–6, 7, 131
Pribram, Francis, 81
Prices, exchange ratios, 20–23, 26–27, 90, 105–106
  economic calculation and, 129–131
Privatdozent (private lecturer), 55–56, 57–58, 78
Production, 91–92, 128
Property, 31–32
Psychology, economics and, 27–28, 71, 124–126
  psychoanalytical movement, 77, 78
Pythagoras, 141

Reisch, Richard, 50
Reisman, George, 4
Returns, increasing/diminishing, law of, 127
Ricardo, David, 11–13, 22, 30, 48, 60, 125

Rockefeller (Laura Spelman) Foundation, 81
Rothbard, Murray N., 4

Sax, Emil, 31–32
Schmoller, Gustav, 34–35, 38–40, 64–66, 67
Schüller, Richard, 74
Schumpeter, Josef, 73
Schütz, Alfred, 80
Science, economic, 3, 7–8, 142–144, 152–157
Science, physical, 7–8, 101–102, 137, 142, 144
Sennholz, Hans F., 4
Sennholz, Mary (Homan), 4
Smith, Adam, 12, 101
Socialism, 67, 76, 128–129
Sociology of knowledge, 71
Sombart, Werner, 68–69
Sorel, Georges, 75
Spadaro, Louis M., 4
Statistics, economic, 3, 5
Stein, Lorenz von, 55
Strigl, Richard von, 58, 74, 115
Subjective value. *See* Value
Supply and demand, 18–19, 21–22, 90, 102

Theory, role of, 49, 98–100
Thünen, Johann Heinrich von, 64
Time, 25, 131–133

Understanding, history and, 156
Universalism (collectivism), 125, 147
Universities
    European, 56–57, 77–78
    German, 36–40, 46, 62, 63–64
    Vienna, 40–46, 54, 57, 78–79, 81
Utilitarianism, 63, 123

Vaihinger, Hans, 116
Value
    Austrian theory of, 11–32, 87–104
    complementary goods and, 94–96, 97–98
    cost and, 92–97, 134–136
    Eudaemonism and, 122–124
    exchange and, 12, 20–21, 119, 125–126
    labor, wages and, 29–30, 31–32
    objective value in exchange (price) and, 19, 26, 27, 30, 90
    paradox of, 2, 14–15, 105–107, 112, 148, 151–152
    profitability and, 135
    scales, 14–17, 19
    subjective, 13, 19, 20–21, 26–27, 50, 90, 105–136, 152
    use, 12–15
    See also Final utility
Van Sickle, John, 79
Verrijn Stuart, C. A., 111
Vienna
    intellectual climate of, 54–58
    University of, 40–46, 57, 78–79, 81
Voegelin, Eric, 79–80
Voluntarism vs. compulsion, 74–78
    See also Cooperation; Government intervention; Socialism

Wagner, Adolph, 35, 36–38, 67
Walras, Léon, 50, 53, 88
Weber, Max, 66, 117
Wicksell, Knut, 74
Wieser, Friedrich von, 2, 11, 14, 19, 29, 30, 51, 54, 56, 59, 70–72, 74, 91
Winternitz, Emanuel, 80

Zuckerkandl, Robert, 74

About the Publisher

The Foundation for Economic Education, Inc., was established in 1946 by Chamber of Commerce executive Leonard E. Read for the purpose of explaining the philosophy of the free market, private property, and limited government. Ludwig von Mises served as FEE's economic adviser from its founding until his death in 1973.

The Foundation publishes books, booklets, and an award-winning monthly journal, *The Freeman,* by means of which FEE seeks to interpret economic issues consistently in the light of Austrian economics. Its book catalog lists many important recent works in the broad fields of economics, history, and moral philosophy as well as time-tested classics by such notables as David Hume, Adam Smith, Frederic Bastiat, Alexis de Tocqueville, Carl Menger, Eugen von Böhm-Bawerk, Ludwig von Mises, Friedrich A. Hayek, and Henry Hazlitt. In addition to its publishing program, FEE conducts seminars, sponsors lectures and encourages discussion groups.

FEE is a non-political, non-profit 501(c)(3) tax-exempt organization, supported solely by private contributions and sales of its literature. For further information, please contact: The Foundation for Economic Education, Inc., 30 South Broadway, Irvington-on-Hudson, New York 10533. Telephone (914) 591-7230; fax (914) 591-8910; E-mail: freeman@westnet.com